Mrs. Mary G. Williams

Hugh V. Brown

Look on Page 130 for my Mother

Revd Sarah J. Williams

A

History Of

The

Education Of Negroes

In North Carolina

By

Hugh Victor Brown

Published 1961

IRVING SWAIN PRESS, INC.

303 SOUTH EAST STREET, RALEIGH, NORTH CAROLINA

A
History Of The
Education Of Negroes
In North Carolina

HUGH VICTOR BROWN
Goldsboro
1960

DEDICATION

NATHAN CLARK NEWBOLD

He spent his life aiding North Carolina in rising above the inequities of a poor and unequal system of public education to a high plane of mutual respectability between the races and thus inspired the onward progress of "Universal Education" which has made this state a leader among the states of the South.

With apologies to Daniel Webster, in his peroration on Alexander Hamilton:

> "He smote the dead rock of mutual understanding
>   And an abundance of good will gushed forth;
> He touched the corpse of public lethargy
>   And it sprang to its feet."

For this cause, I dedicate "Education of Negroes in North Carolina" to Nathan Clark Newbold.

ACKNOWLEDGMENT

While dedicating this work to N. C. Newbold, who was largely responsible for my coming to North Carolina, I am profoundly indebted to my first helpmate, Alice Harper Brown, who was my great inspiration from 1919 until her demise in 1948.

I am extremely grateful to many who so generously aided me in searching for and in compiling this material for publication. They include college presidents, college and public librarians, state officials, and local educators.

I am especially grateful to my wife, Elizabeth Bright Brown; to News Argus Editor Henry Belk, who has encouraged me all along the way; to Mrs. Henry Belk, who read most of the manuscript; to Supervisor of Schools, E. A. House (deceased) and Mrs. Dorothy Hardy, who read the final chapters; and to Mrs. Willette B. Starke and Neal A. Stitt who did the typing.

Dr. W. L. Greene, Executive Secretary of the North Carolina Teachers Association and his office staff, Mrs. Della Perry and Miss Tabitha Pettiford were most helpful in making available the mass of Teachers Association source material for the chapter on the North Carolina Teachers Association. To each of them I am deeply grateful.

Let it be my hope that this book may find its way into every public school and be available to every citizen who is interested in universal education; and that every Negro child will remember and respect the sublime heritage which has been the foundation of our educational success in North Carolina as the following pages will attempt to show.

HUGH VICTOR BROWN
Goldsboro, North Carolina
1960

Contents

Education Of Negroes In North Carolina

Chapter V

Pages 49-65

Education in the Era of Newbold—The Jeanes Fund—George Foster Peabody—Annie W. Holland—Phelps-Stokes Fund—Teacher Training—County Training Schools, County summer schools—Rosenwald schools—Division of Negro Education—Standard high schools—G. H. Ferguson, W. A. Robinson and accreditation.

Chapter VI

Pages 66-99

Education and the Colleges—Shaw University—Saint Augustine's College—Biddle, (Now Johnson C. Smith University)—Bennett College—Livingstone College, role of Price and Aggrey-Scotia, (now Barber Scotia College)—Kittrell College—State Institutions: Normal schools, now teachers' colleges, Fayetteville, E. E. Smith; Elizabeth City and P. W. Moore; Winston-Salem and S. G. Atkins; A. and T. College and James B. Dudley; North Carolina College and James E. Shepard.

Chapter VII

Pages 100-112

Special Secondary and Welfare Institutions—Palmer Memorial Institute, Laurinburg Institute; the Colored Orphanage at Oxford—North Carolina State School for the Blind and Deaf—Morrison Training School—Education of Mentally Defectives—State Training School for Girls—O'Berry School, Training of the Mentally Defective.

Chapter VIII

Pages 113-138

Contingent Educational Influences: North Carolina Teachers Association—Agricultural Extension Service—Education of Nurses—Public Welfare.

Chapter IX

Pages 139-155

The Division of Negro Education; Negroes in the State Department—Supervisor of High Schools—Supervisor of Elementary Schools—Supervisors of Special Education: Vocational Agriculture—Trades and Industries—Home Economics.

Introduction

Education Of Negroes In North Carolina

Many times during the earlier years of my career as a teacher and principal and also as an instructor in county and state summer schools, it occurred to me that something should be written to preserve the unfolding development of the education of Negroes in North Carolina. Great conferences of dedicated men and women of both races, called by N. C. Newbold, met from time to time at Shaw University and set the stage for many "next steps" in this almost incredible saga of a race, "Up from Slavery," to a position of respect in the equation of human relations.

I never missed a single one of these conferences and was deeply moved by such men as E. C. Brooks and A. T. Allen, each at one time State Superintendents; Bishop Walls, of the A. M. E. Zion church; E. E. Smith, Principal of Fayetteville State Normal; P. W. Moore, Principal of Elizabeth City State Normal; S. G. Atkins, Principal of Winston-Salem State Normal; and others within and without the state. I could say as an ancient poet, "All of this I saw and much of it I was."

Once I thought of writing about three of these dedicated pioneers and entitling the story, "The Great Triumvirate of Educators": Atkins, Smith and Moore, the three great principals of our remaining normal schools, now all teachers colleges. However, there were other great and dedicated souls, five of whom Mr. Newbold so beautifully portrayed in "Five North Carolina Negro Educators." This production of Mr. Newbold so eclipsed my dream, that I immediately scrapped the "Great Triumvirate" idea, but the obsession to help preserve for posterity the wonderful work of so many consecrated men and women remained with me.

In 1956, I was eligible for retirement, but it was delayed, pending the erection of a long overdue new high school plant. The inspiration to write persisted and when retirement finally came in 1958, I launched into the effort to magnify the wonderful story of the progress of my people in education in North Carolina.

My associates in the field of education had been urging me to write about my own activities, but that would have been worthless except, perhaps, to those immediately around me. Awareness of the fact that changing times often cause us to forget the influences and the agencies which have motivated these changes, I was seized with the inspiration to gather the facts of our educational history in North Carolina and place them in one package for preservation that—"Lest we forget"—unborn generations might tell their children "how we came through." Many today do not know of the influences and many might not wish to give credit where credit is due, but the race is indebted to more people and more influences than it knows about or is willing to admit.

Immediately upon my retirement, I began to do my researches for the story in the chapters which follow. One of the first and many of the subsequent interviews were with Dr. G. H. Ferguson, successor to Mr. N. C. Newbold, as Director of the Negro Division of Education at the State Department. I went through the files in the State Archives and thumbed through the multiplicity of superintendents' reports from Calvin Wiley to Clyde A. Erwin. Of great help and interest was the file on Negro schools and especially the more recent and excellent file of the Newbold papers.

During the winter of 1958-59, I visited every Negro college in the state and received first-hand information of their development. In addition, I spent a good many days in the University library at Chapel Hill where I was cordially received and aided by the librarians there.

My work was interrupted in 1959 as I had an unprecedented recall to my former post as principal when my successor went on a year's leave. However, at the close of that year, June 1960, I resumed my effort with the determination to complete the story for publication.

Although I have tried to cover the field of educational contributions among many individuals, agencies and influences, the whole story cannot be told, for there remains untold the account of the activities of many dedicated men and women which were not preserved in writing and no one living today can give any accurate summation of what was done by them. It is hoped, however, that most of the best contributions will be found chronicled here and will be an inspiration for present students of the subject, to see to it that the best of today is preserved properly for posterity.

H. V. BROWN.

Chapter I

Ante - Bellum Education Of Negroes

As a background for this story of the education of the Negro in North Carolina, it is necessary to establish some basis. That native Africans, taken from their savage state and without any knowledge of their enslavers' language, could have been employed adequately in a continuing ignorance, is difficult to conceive.

For the protection of the masters and their families as well as for profit in the use of slave labor, there had to be some training of the slave.

Of course there was no formal or literary education; certainly no public schooling for slaves nor for their children, but Negroes had to be taught something to fit them into the South's economy. Most of this teaching naturally was of an agricultural and industrial nature, but many slaves learned something about reading and writing (perhaps, mostly in a clandestine manner) and doubtlessly learned much of their captors' culture. It must also be assumed that they gradually acquired something of the English language.

Religious Instruction of Slaves

The African is naturally an emotional human being. Much of his life has been given to ritualistic ceremony even though beclouded with strange superstition and apparent witchcraft. Nevertheless, it was not difficult to turn his untutored mind toward the white man's religion.

Before slavery in New England was discontinued, efforts were made by such leaders as Roger Williams, Cotton Mather, and John Eliot to enlighten the slaves through religious instruction. The Quakers in the North were actively interested in freedom first, religion afterward and, in the South, though some Quakers owned slaves, under the influence of their northern brethren, they later set them free or transported them to Africa. Quaker schools for Negroes in North Carolina existed as early as 1731.

Other religious organizations, especially Methodist, Baptist, and Presbyterian denominations were actively engaged in giving religious instructions to slaves, while Catholics actually admitted slave children into their schools.[1]

Many slaves were members of white Baptist churches in North Carolina and sometimes outnumbered the whites. The Green River Association of Western North Carolina in 1856 showed that for each colored member of the Association 12.7 were white; while the Union Association in Eastern North Carolina showed 1 colored to 2.2 white.

---

1. Charles William Dabney, *Universal Education in the South*, Vol. 1; pp 437-40.

11

The North Carolina Baptists believed it to be a solemn "religious duty" and grave responsibility of masters, preachers, churches, and church memberships to see that the slaves were taught the doctrines of Christianity. The Baptist Convention in 1837 passed resolutions urging ministers to use their influence to have provided in all places of worship ample and comfortable accommodations for the colored part of their congregations.[2]

The Quakers probably did more than any other religious sect toward the education of Negroes in ante-bellum North Carolina as they entered into the teaching of Negroes with a great deal of enthusiasm and are credited with being largely responsible for the most enlightened of the ante-bellum free Negroes.[3]

Industrial or Practical Training

Slavery originally was for agricultural purposes; uses of the plantation system where slaves in droves could be managed by overseers. Yet many of them, applying perhaps some of their native culture and skill, learned the arts of trades and developed an industrial efficiency upon which later education would be built.

Some of the more skilled slave-tradesmen were often hired out by their masters for wages and were able to purchase their freedom. The grandfather of this writer, born in Kentucky in 1829, was a skilled blacksmith and said to have been the best "shoer of race horses" in his section of Kentucky. He is also said to have made enough money shoeing horses to purchase the freedom of his wife, the maternal grandmother of this writer.

Most of the skilled labor before the Civil War (and for a long time thereafter) was done by Negroes. The slave women did the work in the homes and became expert cooks and seamstresses. Many slave men became trusted body guards, horsemen, carriage drivers and held other positions of trust. They were taught reading and a little ciphering.

"As carpenters, brick masons, wheelwrights, blacksmiths, tanners, plasterers, harness workers, shoemakers, furniture makers and mechanics in the shops, they became accomplished at their respective trades."[4]

Literary Training

Of course there was little or no outward show of literary or academic training for Negroes in ante-bellum times. However, a few instances of the sprouting of "genius" are on record as to native ability of slaves.

2. Willie Grier, *North Carolina Baptists and The Negro;* Unpublished Thesis, University of North Carolina, Chapel Hill, N. C., 1944.

3. John Hope Franklin, *The Free Negro in North Carolina*, p 166.

4. Charles William Dabney; *Op. cit.,* p 436.

George Moses Horton, a slave owned by William Horton in Northampton County, was a born poet. He wrote poems for Chapel Hill students who recognized a spark of genius in him. He would dictate verses to student purchasers and some of them began to appear in the University Magazine. James K. Polk, class of 1818 at the University of North Carolina, later to become the 11th president of the United States, was first to encourage Horton in his literary ambitions. His poems were published by Dennis Hearth in Hillsborough 1845 as "The Poetical Works of George Moses Horton."

Horton at one time endeavored to buy his freedom by means of sales of his poems, but was not successful. He later tried to sell himself to Governor Swain, but in this was also unsuccessful.

His last and largest book of poems, entitled, "Naked Genius" was published in 1865 and contained 132 poems, 39 of which were in a previous book. Most of them dealt with the theme of slavery; some of them with war and heroes.[5]

Era of John Chavis In North Carolina

Because of the unique role of John Chavis as a preacher and as a teacher of white students, this section is rightly called, "The Era of John Chavis."

Much doubt existed as to the nativity of John Chavis. Some had him born in the West Indies while others were certain that he was born in Granville County, North Carolina.[6] Of himself, Chavis said that he was a free born American and a revolutionary soldier.[7]

It seems authentic that he went to Oxford, England, from where he was induced to come to America by a student from Connecticut. Because of the rigors of the Connecticut winter, he removed to Virginia, where he is alleged to have attended school at Washington and Lee University at Lexington. His first ministerial duties were performed under the direction of the North Carolina Presbytery in 1805.[8]

Considerable doubt also exists as to the extent of Chavis' education. It was alleged that he was sent to Princeton University to see if a Negro could take collegiate education. In all probabilities, Chavis did go to Princeton and took private lessons from the President of the University. Suffice it to say, he was educated above the status of his peers.[9]

5. Mattie Temple Tatum Lakin, *George Moses Horton—Slave Poet;* Unpublished Thesis, North Carolina College, Durham, N. C., pp 7, 23.

6. G. C. Shaw, *John Chavis,* 1763-1838. pp 2, 4.

7. Benjamin Brawley, *Negro Builders and Heroes.* p 48.

8. Stephen B. Weeks, "The Ante-Bellum Preacher," *Southern Workman;* Hampton Institute, February, 1914.

9. G. C. Shaw, *Op. cit.* pp 7, 10.

Although Chavis was well known as a preacher, it was in teaching that he was better known and is to be remembered. He was said to have the best school in the state. Some of his students, by their rise and development, seem to justify this claim and became leaders in North Carolina. Among them are: Willie P. Mangum, who represented the State in the United States Senate, Priestly Hinton, Archibald and John Henderson, sons of Chief Justice Henderson, Governor Charles Manly, the Reverend William Harris, Dr. James L. Wortham, the Edwardses, the Etows, the Hargraves, all prominent North Carolinians and many others who became lawyers, preachers, physicians, and teachers.[10]

Chavis taught at various times in Chatham, Wake, Orange, and Granville Counties. His schools served as high schools and academies for the section in which they were located and as preparatory schools for the University of North Carolina.

Stephen B. Weeks, a son-in-law of Senator Mangum, lists the following leading North Carolinians as having been among Chavis's students: Priestly H. Mangum, brother of Senator Mangum and himself a lawyer of distinction, Abram Rancher, who became Governor of New Mexico, and James H. Horner, founder of The Horner School.[11]

Thus far mention has been made only of Chavis' teaching of white students, but he also conducted schools for free Negroes. At first he taught them together, but complaints dictated otherwise and he therefore conducted schools separately for free Negroes.

There is no way of knowing how many free Negro children were taught by John Chavis between 1808 and some date in the 1830's when he retired from active teaching. His teaching must have touched many in view of the fact that his school for free Negroes was conducted for almost thirty years.

It is impossible, moreover, to make an estimate of the effect of the teachings of John Chavis on the social status of the free Negro in ante-bellum North Carolina. This status was doubtless raised through the efforts of his free Negro students, who for more than a generation, were inspired by his lofty idealism and his insistence on the possibility that every individual might better his own condition. Perhaps it was elevated even more by the figure of John Chavis, teacher not only of free Negro children, but also of white children! As a teacher of such persons as Willie and Preston Mangum (whom he affectionately called "My Sons"), Archibald and John Henderson, Charles Manly, and James Wortham, he was a negation of much for which the white community stood in its attitude toward the free

10. *Ibid.*, pp 14, 15.

11. Stephen B. Weeks, *Op. cit.*
John Hope Franklin, *Op. cit.* pp 171-172.

14

Negro. Intellectually, he was inferior to few North Carolinians. The lively interest which he displayed in all public questions was equal to that manifested by most leaders within the State. He was, indeed, a citizen of North Carolina and a participant in its intellectual as well as in its political developments.[12]

Chavis was entertained in the homes of his white friends, who profited by his preaching and intellectual discourses upon the issues of the times—and apparently respected his opinions and general intelligence. It is difficult to understand how a man of his race could have been so accepted instead of being expected to occupy the role of a slave. However, his demeanor was always in keeping with his intellectual philosophy and thus commanded the respect which, in the times in which he lived could be viewed as unusual.[13]

Summary

Education of the Negro prior to the Civil War consisted of practical necessity in implementing the life of the uncivilized captive into the economic life of the South. He had to be trained to meet the needs of his owner. More humane consideration dictated the teaching of the Christian religion which the Negro slave with little difficulty because of his emotional nature easily and quickly absorbed. From the background of his native ability and African culture, the Negro soon learned much of the mechanics of industrial activity which developed into skilled trades. Consciously or unconsciously his masters were contributing to his education and specifically teaching him to read and to figure.

Incidentally, while religious sects were instilling Christian religious principles into the hearts of the slaves, they too were leading his mind to a fountain of learning.

John Chavis was unique in his contribution to the education of the Negro in ante-bellum North Carolina, but records are lacking in a contribution made by many slave holders and their families who, doubtless like "Little Eva" in Uncle Tom's Cabin, paved the way by which many a slave caught the "crumbs of education" which fell from the white man's table.

---

12. M. Grant Batey, John Chavis' Contribution to Education in North Carolina; *Unpublished Thesis, North Carolina College, Durham, North Carolina,* 1954. p 34.

13. *Ibid.,* p 34.

Chapter II

Education During The Transition Period

Perhaps many people of the South, living at the time of the 1954 Supreme Court decision in the integration cases, had they been living in 1863, would have said that the Negro was not ready for emancipation.

Judging by the confused circumstances of the times, the legal question of what slaves were affected by the Emancipation Act, as well as the implementation of the freedmen's relationships with their erstwhile masters, the country itself was not wholly ready for the answer to the question of what to do with the slaves or what the freedmen would do with themselves when they would be free.

There were efforts which showed that many righteous people were preparing for the emergency which they saw was inevitable.

The New England Freedmen's Aid Society started education of the Negro in South Carolina in 1862 when thirty-one men and women arrived there as teachers. In North Carolina the chaplains of Northern regiments took an early interest in the education of Negroes. The American Missionary Association followed in the wake of the activities of the army chaplains.

The first day-schools were set up at New Bern in July, 1863; one year later there were schools at Beaufort, Washington, Plymouth, and at other places with 3,000 students and 66 teachers.[1]

The Emancipation Proclamation gave legal freedom to the slaves except those in the states which had been reclaimed by the Union, but it actually freed none who were not reached by Union armies. However, it settled forever the safety of fugitives escaping to Union army lines—and they came by the thousands to wherever the Union armies were.

They were cared for as best they could be; located in camps and on abandoned plantations. They seemed more anxious for schools than for food. Volunteer ladies (Northern teachers) offered their services. Freedmen's societies were organized. Religious organizations sent ministers and teachers to various points.

The American Missionary Association rapidly extended its work and established early schools at New Bern and on Roanoke Island.

Schools followed in the wake of the Union armies. A Mr. Coan, representing the American Missionary Association, was in Wilmington with teachers as the army entered there. About one thousand pupils reported themselves in less than one week after the arrival of the army. Evening schools were provided for adults.[2]

---

1. John Hope Franklin, *From Slavery To Freedom*, p. 272.

2. S. W. Green, *History of American Missionary Association*, 1874, p. 2.

Colonize or Educate?

In the midst of the slave era, many wise and liberal slave holders held mixed opinions as to the righteousness or sin of the slave system. In the North, slavery was early recognized as unprofitable and almost as early it was abandoned. Whereas, the North condemned the South as being unrighteous to maintain slavery, the North could take no righteous credit to itself mainly because it was the economic motive which impelled the giving up of the slave system.

On the other hand, the South did not awaken to the enormous cost of slave labor and the consequent economic loss until slavery was ended. It then found production of its main resources, cotton and corn, far in excess of the same under slave labor.

George Washington is said to have willed freedom to all his slaves at the death of his wife and Thomas Jefferson is said to have done likewise. The fact that in 1860 there were 30,463 free Negroes in North Carolina indicates that many wise and benevolent slave holders had rid themselves of the curse of slavery.

How to implement the free Negro into the South's social system was as much of a problem as that of keeping him a slave had been. Some colonization had been effected; notably in the country of Liberia, Africa, about the time of the administration of President James Monroe.

President Lincoln, himself, considered a plan of shipping the freed Negroes out of the country, if they could be persuaded to go willingly,[3] but fate nullified any such consideration.

It could hardly be expected that the Negroes would have been willing to leave the only home they had known and, as expressed in later years by the poet, Paul Lawrence Dunbar, they were not going until "God said, 'Forward march'!"

It is difficult for us of this generation to comprehend fully just how smoothly or confusedly the South evolved from a slave economy to that of a paid labor system. That some colonization ensued was true in North Carolina and wherever Union armies conquered; for "refugees" flocked into the army camps and were cared for by the soldiers.

To meet the emergency created by the Emancipation Proclamation, Departments were set up to superintend Negro affairs. This provision was the forerunner of the Freedmen's Bureau. Major General George J. Carney, A.I.M., was Superintendent General of Negro Affairs of the Department of Virginia and North Carolina. The headquarters of the Eastern District in North Carolina was at New Bern, the largest rendezvous of colored people in the district. Other points of concentration in the Eastern District were Beaufort, Washington, Roanoke Island, Plymouth and Hatteras Banks.

With the heavy concentration of refugees in and around New Bern the consequent shortage of food, and with little or no sanita-

---

3. Richard N. Current, *The Lincoln Nobody Knows*, 1958, pp 221-22.

tion, disease was bound to ensue. During the winter of 1864, smallpox raged and in the autumn yellow fever followed. In February,
fully fifty persons per week died of smallpox and in October nearly
as many per day died of yellow fever.[4]

Roanoke Island

A Negro colony was started on Roanoke Island in May, 1863, under Chaplain Horace James, Assistant Commander of the Bureau
of Refugees, Freedmen, and Abandoned Lands. Major General
J. G. Foster, who was then commanding the Department of Virginia
and North Carolina, proposed to settle colored people on the un-
occupied lands and furnish them with agricultural implements and
mechanical tools to train and educate them for a free and independent community.

Colored soldiers were first recruited on Roanoke Island on June
19, 1863. The removal of the vigorous young men to the army
converted the colony into a veritable asylum for the wives and
children of soldiers, and also for the aged and infirm. Here the
children might be educated, and all, both young and old, might be
trained for freedom and its responsibilities when war should end.
Chaplain James notes in his Annual Report:

> I went north in June 1863, under the orders from Gen-
> eral Foster, to procure materials and implements with
> which to furnish the projected colony with an outfit, and
> in a few weeks raised in New England and New York be-
> tween eight and nine thousand dollars. It was most cheer-
> fully given, and the donations were accompanied with
> many expressions of good-will towards the work, and of
> hearty interest in the colored people. Especially did the
> Freedmen's Associations at Boston and New York render
> efficient aid.[5]

Beaufort

The American Missionary Association sent the Reverend George
W. Greene to start a school in a section in Carteret County where
two creeks, Adam's and Clumfort's, flow north into the Neuse
River. Nearly a thousand colored people settled along the course
and near the mouth of these creeks. The New England Freedmen's
Aid Society sent a Mrs. Carrie E. Croome from Boston to aid in
teaching the Negroes, but the school was burned by Confederate
guerrillas and the teacher threatened if she persisted in schooling
Negroes. However, the Missionary Association sent the same agent
back with materials to rebuild the school.[6]

---

4. Rev. Horace James, "Annual Report of the Superintendent of Negro
   Affairs in North Carolina History and Management of Freedmen Up
   To June 1, 1856," p. 16.

5. *Ibid.*, pp 21, 23.

6. *Ibid.*, pp 20, 21.

Plymouth

Schools for Negroes in Plymouth, N. C., were in existence in 1863 and were conducted by the chaplain of the 25th Massachusetts Regiment. The Negroes were showing great interest in obtaining knowledge when the town was retaken by the Confederates and the Negroes remanded back to slavery in the interior.

Washington, N. C.

The fall of Plymouth caused evacuation of the army at Washington and the consequent loss of the schools which had been set up there. Samuel M. Leathers, superintendent of the land development, had started cultivation and had erected comfortable homes. Pioneer teachers, Miss Fannie Graves, Miss Sarah T. Dickinson, and Miss Anna M. Seavey, had done excellent work in setting up the schools in a community greatly prejudiced against the movement, because it was made up so largely of persons born in North Carolina.[7]

A summary of this Annual Report of the superintendent of Negro Affairs shows that the first schools established in North Carolina under the Bureau were opened in New Bern on July 23, 1863 in two colored churches. By January 1, 1864, the number of pupils was 1,500. By July 1864 the number had reached 3,000. The total number of schools in the District was nineteen day schools and eight evening schools. The New England Freedmen's Aid Society had commissioned 20 teachers; the American Missionary Association, 22; the National Freedmen's Relief Association, 20 white, 4 colored; Independent 2; total 68, of which 12 were male; 56 female.

One of the colored teachers was Robert Morrow, a sergeant in the 1st North Carolina Heavy Artillery (colored troops). He had been the body servant of the Confederate General Pettigrew; had been with him at West Point and Chapel Hill, but deserted and escaped to the Union lines. He had a decent education, and was an enthusiastic and excellent teacher although of pure African blood.[8]

When the Negroes had been assured that the war was at an end, many who had flocked to the cities returned to the plantations, their former homes. They showed a great desire to learn. Schools were set up by the northern educational bodies in Wilmington, Goldsboro, Kinston, and different points along the Cape Fear River. Army chaplains cooperated with these organizations and for a time were the teachers.

Significant is the fact that Shaw University was begun by a former army chaplain, Henry Martin Tupper, December 1, 1865, less than eight months from the close of the war.[9]

---

7. *Ibid.*, pp 36, 37.

8. *Ibid.*, p. 43.

9. W. N. Hartshorn, *Era of Progress and Promise*, p. 87.

The story of Shaw University and activities of the various missionary groups at other institutions will be told in a later chapter, but suffice it to say that the education of the Negro is profoundly indebted to the missionaries who came from the North to answer the challenge, "was the Negro ready for emancipation?"

Long, long after, in 1927, Dr. S. G. Atkins, President of the North Carolina Teachers Association, at that time in his address at Goldsboro, said these words:

> The Negro people would have been in a sorry plight, but for the memorable work of the churches and missionary societies of the North. The splendid institutions founded and maintained by missionary endeavor . . . were teaching and training centers that started our people on their way to the promised land.
>
> Let us not forget those noble missionary educators who were sent to organize and man these fine institutions founded by northern missionary benevolence: Tupper, at Shaw, Matoon at Biddle, Smith and Smedes at St. Augustine's, Steel at Bennett, and Dorland at Scotia. The Negro people of the State owe these missionary societies and these men an inestimable debt. They produced most of the men and women who were prepared to promote the work of the new era and to carry forward the programs which were unfolding with such remarkable rapidity to this day.[10]

Attitudes of the Whites in The Transition Period

It could hardly be expected for the white people of North Carolina to be enthusiastic or even interested at all in the education of Negroes in the Period of Transition from slavery to reconstruction. How could they be interested when their own economic survival was in a state of confusion? With their slaves freed, their currency worthless, and their civil government uncertain, there was not much that the white people could do even for themselves.

Yet, it must go down to their credit that the lands, upon which the first institutions for Negroes were built, were sold to these institutions by the white people of Norh Carolina. Doubtless, too, many white people, even in this uncertain period, contributed something financially and perhaps in materials, toward the erection and the maintenance of these early institutions for Negroes.

On the other hand, a great deal of hostility to educational activities existed. Dr. Tupper, who founded Shaw University, was forced to hide in a field all night with his wife to escape the wrath of hostile forces while he was establishing his institution.[11]

---

10. S. G. Atkins, "President's Address, N. C. Teachers Association," Goldsboro 1927, p. 9.

11. C. F. Graves, *The Story of The Negro Baptists of North Carolina*, p. 17.

The status of the confused inter-racial relationships made the State a fertile field for the operations of outside influences. As early as the spring of 1865 northern Negroes came into the State and began to petition for equal rights. One of them was J. W. Hood, of Connecticut, whose activities throughout the reconstruction era will be noted in a later chapter. Another Negro was James H. Harris, of Ohio. These men, among others, held a series of meetings and passed resolutions in moderate and well chosen language in which they sought protection and opportunity for education and sought to abolish discrimination before the law. Their activities developed into an Equal Rights League.[12]

Summary

The transition period between slavery and freedom of the Negro in the United States roughly coincides with the period of the civil war. As has been stated, some education, even formal training, antedated the period of the Civil War, but most of this education was industrial or functional to fit the slave to the South's economy.

With the issuance of the Emancipation Proclamation and the subsequent enlisting of Negroes into Union Armies, education took on a new emphasis. Union Army chaplains had Negro refugees on their hands and whether the chaplains desired it or not, they set up schools for the Negroes even if the motive were in self defense. Of a certainty many of these devout chaplains and even some army officers were moved with righteous motives with the sight of the pitiful, ignorant, and defenseless hordes which escaped to their lines.

Early in the war General Butler, of the famous "contraband of war" decision, had personally sought to free the Negroes who were in the wake of his conquests. Lincoln disavowed Butler's activities with regard to slaves and ordered any slaves escaping to Union lines to be returned to their masters.

The Emancipation Proclamation ended all doubt as to the status of slaves escaping to Union Armies. Thereafter they came by the thousands and there was nothing for the armies to do but to take care of them as best they could.

Here was set up the Bureau of Negro Affairs and Abandoned Lands, the forerunner of the Freedmen's Bureau, the purpose of which was to implement the ex-slave into a community of civic citizenship.

Missionary associations from the North moved in and in cooperation with the army chaplains set up schools wherever they could conveniently do so. Most of the teachers were from the North and were white; yet a few educated Negroes also were secured to teach.

With the close of the war and the passage of the Thirteenth Amendment which abolished slavery, education of the Negro pro-

---

12. J. G. DeRoulach Hamilton, *Reconstruction in North Carolina*, 1914.

21

gressed rapidly and although hostile elements often militated against the efforts, many white people were receptive to the inevitable consequence of emancipation and made what contribution they could make, in selling land sites for schools and often making contributions through religious organizations and, doubtless, personal contributions which are known only to God.

During this transition period, Shaw University was born and although Dr. Tupper endured many hardships, he could not have succeeded without some local approval and help from local white people. However, the Negro people of North Carolina are forever indebted to the heroic efforts of northern missionary workers who gave so much, sometimes even their lives, that the education of the Negro might be assured.

Chapter III

Reconstruction And Recovery

The period discussed in this chapter is one of the most difficult in the history of the education of the Negro in North Carolina; and indeed in the entire South. Equally it is a sad and unfortunate period in our entire history, for it initiated and aggravated the causes of much of the inter-racial feelings and misunderstanding which exist even down to this day.

Of the causes and the consequences of the regrettable activities of the period, this story avoids any evaluation except to say that the tensions of the times make it difficult to conceive how any appreciable progress in education was made. Even among the whites, education was in a deplorable condition. In many sections of the state, there were no schools for either race. The schools of higher learning among the whites, even the University of North Carolina, had been forced to close their doors, due to the financial conditions of the times. Conservatives, in control of the State Government between 1865 and 1868, abolished the office of state superintendent of common schools.

However, in 1869, the legislature passed a school law providing for separate schools for whites and Negroes, a four months' school term, and a township tax to support the four months' schools of the township but failed to make provision therefor. The Superintendent of Public Instruction, under the Public School Law of 1869 was S. S. Ashley and his assistant was a Negro, J. W. Hood. At the time the enrollment in the public schools was 49,999, nearly half of which was Negroes in separate schools.[1]

As for the welfare status of the Negro, two powerful forces arose to influence his progress in freedom while a third element was torn with mixed emotions as to its role relative to the educational status of the colored people.

First, there was that element which advocated equal rights and political activity as natural consequences of emancipation. This element was made up largely of northerners who preyed upon the weaknesses of the South, in defeat, and of some southerners who saw an opportunity to enhance their own political ambitions upon the enfranchisement and ignorance of the ex-slaves. The former were known as "Carpet baggers" and the latter as "scalawags."

Although some Negroes were well enough educated and actually served in both state and national legislatures, as well as in many other governmental functions, a vast majority of them obviously were not prepared for the art of statecraft nor of governmental responsibilities at a time so soon following their emancipation.

---

1. Hugh Talmage Lefler and Albert Ray Newsome, *North Carolina*, pp. 489, 500.

BISHOP JAMES W. HOOD

Assistant Superintendent of Public Instruction in 1859.

The second and far more salutary force which greatly influenced and promoted real progress of the Negroes was that of the Freedmen's Bureau and the various missionary organizations which promoted educational development, without emphasizing political or equal rights for Negroes.

The Freedmen's Bureau

By Act of Congress, July 2, 1864, a department was set up to supervise and to provide for the welfare of the newly emancipated slaves. This department (referred to in Chapter I) was called the Bureau of Freedmen, Refugees, and Abandoned Lands. Its agents were directed not only to provide for the welfare of the ex-slaves, but also to establish schools for them. It continued to operate until the actual establishment of the Freedmen's Bureau, March 3, 1865.
The main objectives of the Freedmen's Bureau were:
1. To aid the destitute, without encouraging dependence
2. To protect the freedmen from injustice
3. To assist the freedmen in obtaining employment at fair wages
4. To encourage education
At the outset, considerable sums were appropriated for educational work and these were augmented by later acts as the schools increased from 63 in 1865 to 431 in 1869 and from 5,623 pupils to 20,227.[2]

The White Factor

The third factor influencing Negro education and welfare was that of the white people themselves. As stated before, the whites were in dire financial circumstances and unable to do much even for themselves, but there is perhaps little doubt that there were many whites who realized the necessity of education for the ex-slaves, but were hindered by actual inability to do so as well as hostility toward the problem.
Following the close of the war, the North Carolina white Baptists recognized their duty and obligation toward the freed men and were ready to help in forming church associations, day schools, and Sunday Schools, but the development of the so-called "Carpet-bag" rule caused them to lessen their spirit toward helping the Negroes.[3]

Missionary Associations

By far the greatest boost given the education of the Negro during the Reconstruction Period came from the northern missionary organizations and the various local and state religious denominations of Negroes. Without the activities of these organizations, progress

---

2. J. B. De Roulhac Hamilton, *Reconstruction in North Carolina*, pp. 295-315.

3. Willie Grier, *North Carolina Baptists and the Negro*; unpublished thesis, University of North Carolina, 1944. pp. 78, 113.

in education of Negroes would have been very slow. In every section of the state, some type of institution was established by a church or an association of churches.

Many of these schools were perhaps misnamed; academy, seminary, college, or university, but despite the probable misnomer, they served a great purpose at a time when the State was unable to do its part. Most of these institutions have served their purpose and have now been disbanded, but the more well established are still alive and constitute great pillars of strength in the education of Negroes today.

A survey of the list of national missionary organizations credited with the establishing of many institutions for the Negro race throughout the South is indeed illuminating if not profound. Their activities were superseded by several great educational funds, which will be the subject of a later chapter.

As has already been indicated, the Freedmen's Bureau, superseding the Bureau of Refugees, Freedmen, and Abandoned Lands, had sponsored schools during the transition period between the issuance of the Emancipation Proclamation and the close of the Civil War. The missionary organizations had started their work and cooperated with the Bureau in supplying teachers. Their activities continued long after the close of the war and, to some extent, down to the twentieth century when they were gradually relinquished with the coming of "Universal Education" and Charles B. Aycock.

The American Baptist Home Mission Society contributed to many small Baptist schools and is today custodian for the endowment funds of Shaw University.[4]

Two other institutions, Waters Institute, 1886[5] at Winton and New Bern Collegiate and Industrial Institute, at New Bern, in 1902 were sponsored by the American Baptist Home Mission Society.[6]

The American Missionary Association set up Washburn Seminary at Beaufort in 1863;[7] Gregory Institute, Wilmington, 1865;[8] Peabody Academy, Troy, 1880;[9] Lincoln Academy, Kings Mountain, 1892;[10] and The Joseph K. Brick School, Bricks, in 1895.[11]

The African Methodist Episcopal Church, strictly a Negro denomination, set up Kittrell College at Kittrell in 1886.[12]

---

4. The Shaw Bulletin, Shaw University, July 1957, p. 21.

5. W. N. Hartshorne, *An Era of progress and promise, 1863-1910*, p. 124.

6. J. A. Whitted, *History of Negro Baptists.* pp. 180, 181.

7. W. N. Hartshorne, *op. cit.,* p. 148.

8. *Ibid.,* p. 160.

9. *Ibid.,* p. 159.

10. *Ibid.,* p. 157.

11. *Ibid.,* p. 147.

12. *Ibid.,* p. 278.

The African Methodist Episcopal Zion Church, also strictly a Negro denomination, set up Livingstone College at Salisbury in 1882; Eastern Academy at New Bern in 1895; and Edenton Normal and Industrial School at Edenton in 1901.[13]

The Christian Missionary Alliance founded the Mary B. Mullen School at Ayr, N. C., in 1907 and the Lovejoy Mission Institute at Tryon in 1895;[14] and The Daniel Hand Fund endowed Douglas Academy in 1907.[15] High Point Normal and Industrial School at High Point was set up by the Friends Society in 1893.[16] The Protestant Episcopal Church in cooperation with the Freedmen's Bureau, established Saint Augustine's College in Raleigh in 1867[17] and Saint Michael's Church and Industrial School at Charlotte in 1882[18]

The Freedmen's Aid Society of the Methodist Church established Bennett College in Greensboro in 1874.[19] The Board of Missions For Freedmen of the Presbyterian Church operated and aided the following institutions: Biddle (now Johnson C. Smith) University at Charlotte, 1867; Scotia Seminary (now Barber Scotia College) at Concord, 1870; Albion Academy at Franklinton, 1878; Mary Potter Seminary at Oxford, 1893; Dayton Academy at Carthage, 1883; Red Stone Academy at Lumberton and Sarah Lincoln Academy at Aberdeen in 1896.[20] The Freedmen's Board of the United Presbyterian Church established Henderson Institute at Henderson in 1890 and Townsville Mission at Townsville in 1904.[21] The Synodical Conference of North America (Luthern) established Immanuel Lutheran College at Greensboro in 1903.[22]

Because of numerical superiority, the Baptists established more secondary schools than any other religious denomination. Almost every district association (and there were many) endeavored to set up a school. Doubtless, the establishment of some of these institutions was motivated by selfish ambitions and unwarranted competition,[23] but it is to the eternal credit of these pioneers that they endeavored to provide secondary education for their children when there was no other means by which it could be provided.

13. *Ibid.*, p. 290.

14. *Ibid.*, p. 266.

15. *Ibid.*, p. 167.

16. *Ibid.*, p. 260.

17. *Ibid.*, p. 253.

18. *Ibid.*, p. 257.

19. *Ibid.*, p. 170.

20. *Ibid.*, p. 200.

21. *Ibid.*, p. 216.

22. Rev. William H. Kampschmitt, M. A., President Immanuel Lutheran College, Greensboro, N. C. Letter to the Author; October 1958.

23. J. A. Whitted, *Op. cit.*, pp. 83, 84.

A list of these schools follows: Hyde Institute, Belhaven; Zion Academy, Wadesboro; Thompson Institute, Lumberton; Neuse River Institute, Weldon; Tar River Institute, Greenville; Madison Institute, Madison; Ayden Institute, Ayden; Shiloh Institute, Warrenton; Reedy Creek Institute, Littleton; Claremont Institute, Claremont; Roanoke Institute, Elizabeth City; Oak Grove Institute, Jacksonville; New Bern Eastern Institute, Brownsville; McDaniel Institute, Kinston; Burgaw High School, Burgaw; Union Academy, Clinton; Pee Dee Institute, Hamlet; Hodges Institute, West Clinton; Johnston Academy, Smithfield; Garysburg High School, Garysburg; Faison Institute, Faison; New Hill School, Chapel Hill; Middle Ground Institute, Williamston; Higgs Institute, Parmele; Cedar Grove Academy, Roxboro; Scotland Neck Institute, Scotland Neck; Albemarle Training School, Bienton; New Middle Swamp Institute, Corapeake; Dallas Institute, Dallas; Waters Normal Institute, Winton; New Bern Industrial Institute, New Bern; Bertie Academy, Windsor; Rich Square Academy, Rich Square; Girls Training School, Franklinton; Wharton Institute, Charlotte, and perhaps some other lesser known schools all of which, except Roanoke Institute, have either been discontinued or have been assumed by the State.[24] The Free Will Baptist denomination operated a school at Kinston, Kinston College, which has been discontinued.

Many ambitious individuals endeavored to found schools independent of any associations, but such schools found it extremely difficult to survive. Notable was the effort of the Rev. M. L. Latta[25] who established a school called "Latta University" at West Raleigh in 1892. The Reverend Mr. Latta travelled all over the North and as far west as San Francisco in search of funds, but the institution never attained a solvent footing and consequently was discontinued.

The Greatest Needs of the Period

Granting that the need of spirit and desire for education had already been met, the greatest remaining needs of the time were, first, funds to set up and operate schools; and secondly, trained teachers to instruct the pupils.

Public Funds

The Public Law of 1869 had authorized a township tax to provide for a four months' school, but this provision was violated in many counties. The Legislature of 1871 passed a state tax of six and two thirds cents on each $100 valuation of property and twenty cents on each poll for public schools, but the proceeds in each county were to be used by that county. If revenue was insufficient to sup-

---

24. C. F. Graves, *Story of the Negro Baptists in North Carolina*, p. 33.

25. M. L. Latta, *Story of My Life and Work*, p. 80.

port the four months' school, the county commissioners were prohibited from levying a special tax to supply the deficiency.[26]

Private Funds; The Peabody Fund

George Peabody, a wealthy merchant of Boston, in 1867 created a trust fund of One Million Dollars and added another million in 1869 to:

Encourage and assist educational effort in those portions of our beloved and common country which have suffered from the destructive ravages of war.

The policy of the fund was to cooperate with state authority by contributing a sum of $300 for an enrollment of 100 pupils; $600 for an enrollment of 200; and $1,000 for an enrollment of 300 pupils. The fund required a term of 10 months and, although applied to Negroes as well as to whites, the Negroes usually received two-thirds of the amount allowed to white schools. In 1871, Washington had a white school with 132 pupils and a colored school with 451 pupils. The Peabody Fund granted $300 to the white and $600 to the colored school. Beaufort, with a white school of 150 pupils, was promised $450 if it continued ten months and $400 for the colored school of 200 pupils on the same condition. Kinston colored school received $300 in 1871 at the height of the Civil Rights agitation in Congress.[27]

Dr. Barnas Sears, President of Brown University, resigned his presidency to become agent for the fund. He journeyed all over the South conferring with leading citizens and made a careful study of existing schools and devoted himself toward understanding the needs of the southern people. Dr. Sears' recommendations to the Peabody Board, based upon his survey of conditions and needs of southern schools were far-reaching in the future activities and practices of the fund.

They included the following:

1. The disposition of the fund would be confined to public schools.

2. It would render aid where large numbers could be gathered and a model system organized.

3. Preference would be given to communities having wide influence upon surrounding areas.

4. That the power and efficiency of a limited number of schools in a given locality be considered rather than a multiplication of schools that would languish for want of sufficient support.

5. That efforts be made to improve state systems of education.

6. That state normal schools be regarded with special favor.

---

26. Hugh Talmage Lefler and Albert Ray Newsome, *op. cit.*, p. 502.

27. Edgar W. Knight, *Public Education in North Carolina*, p. 277.

7. That special attention be given to training of females for primary schools, rather than to general culture of young men in college.

8. That preparation of colored teachers be encouraged in regular normal schools.

9. The appointment of state superintendents, formation of state associations of teachers, and the publication of periodicals for the improvement of teachers.

These recommendations were accepted by the Peabody Board and became the policy of the fund. Benefits were confind to public schools and in no case were they to meet the entire cost.[28]

Lefler and Newsome say that the Peabody Fund did not meet with much response in North Carolina, but did stimulate some local school support, helped to establish excellent town schools, and tended to allay the bitterness and hatred of the times.[29]

The State received $22,000 from the fund in 1868. Larger towns were the first to meet its conditions, aid being based upon subscriptions of at least two to three times the amount appropriated by the fund. In addition, an average standard of attendance was required. Wilmington was offered $1,500 on condition it raised $3,000; New Bern, $1,000 if it raised $2,500; Raleigh and Charlotte were to receive $1,000 each on the same conditions.

A Negro school at Warrenton received $400; Fayetteville, $300; Oxford, $300 from June, 1872 to July, 1873. In 1884 a Negro school at Beaufort and one at Tarboro received $300 each; one at Fayetteville, $50 and $100 for teachers institutes. In 1875, a Negro school at Charlotte received $600; Fayetteville and Tarboro $450 each. October, 1875, to the summer of 1876, a Negro school at Fayetteville and one at Charlotte, $450 each; a Negro school at Tarboro and one at Raleigh, $300 each.

In 1876, the fund appropriated to Fayetteville and Charlotte $250 and $450 respectively. From 1878 until the final disposition of the fund, North Carolina shared in its distribution. In 1878, about $4,500 was distributed to graded schools, normal schools, and other educational work. It took into account the need of preparation of teachers by aiding in teachers' institutes and in granting scholarships to normal schools.

One of the greatest contributions of the Peabody Fund was its influence in lessening prejudice and hostility toward Negro schools. Despite the confusion and misunderstanding of the times, southern whites gave $110 million dollars between 1870 and 1900 for Negro education.[30]

---

28. W. N. Hartshorne, *op. cit.*, pp. 542, 543.

29. Hugh Lefler and Albert Newsome, *op. cit.*, p. 505.

30. Edgar W. Knight, *op cit.*, p. 291.

Federal Aid

As in later years, there was some advocacy for Federal funds, but aside from those funds coming under the Morrill Act for State Colleges of Agriculture, there was no Federal relief. Revenue from many counties could not keep schools more than three months a year and pay teachers more than $25 per month. Major Robert Bingham, of the Bingham School, speaking before the National Education Association convention in Washington, D. C., February 15, 1884, said:

> With national aid for ten years we can manage illiteracy both among colored and white, but if we continue the unequal struggle for these most germinant years without support, people will become discouraged and there is danger that a darkness will envelope a people who will only need temporary aid to put them where they can and will provide for themselves.[31]

The Need For Trained Teachers

The second great need of education during the Reconstruction Period was an ample supply of trained teachers. This great need among advocates for education for whites was recognized in the early days of Reconstruction as a serious problem, due to the loss of their academies and the closing of the University. Obviously, it was a more serious problem among the advocates of education for the Negroes. Despite the sending of teachers from the North by the various missionary organizations, the problem of teacher supply was almost critical.

Shaw University, in the years immediately following the close of the war, made great strides toward supplying teachers for the rapidly growing number of schools, but the demand far out-distanced the supply. The same was true in the western part of the state with Biddle University at Charlotte.

Major Bingham, continuing his address before the convention of the National Education Association, referred to above, said:

> The states can do more than they are doing in the way of summer institutes lasting only four or five weeks; and unless continual normal training is provided for in some way at points numerous enough to be reached at small cost and without tuition fees, national aid will lose one half of its value and probably two thirds of its value, for lack of teachers to administer it who know methods as well as subjects.
>
> Such colored (sic) men and women as General Armstrong at Hampton and Dr. Tupper of Shaw University should be enabled to train their own race; and if the pay were sufficient, by degrees our best white people who, in

---

31. Robert Bingham, Address, National Education Association, February 15, 1884, National Aid to Education, *The New South*, February, 1884, p. 20.

31

many localities, have labored for years in the religious training of the colored people in Sunday Schools would become interested in their public work and such schools, like mission schools in heathen lands, without disturbing the social relations of teachers and taught, would do much to secure harmony and to cultivate kindness between races.[32]

What was known as normal training of teachers had existed as "departments" in the academies and colleges of white institutions. The pattern was followed in the Negro schools. Summer normals, sometimes called institutes, had been improving the professional growth of teachers, and became the forerunners of the state normal schools. The Peabody Fund favored state normal schools rather than departments in the colleges and academies[33] and upon its recommendation, normal schools began to appear.

Normal Schools

In order to meet the great need for trained teachers, the North Carolina Legislature of 1877 passed an act to provide normal schools for both races. The first such institution for Negroes was accordingly established at Fayetteville in 1877.[34]

Other state normal schools for Negroes were established as follows: Plymouth Normal at Plymouth, 1881; Slater Normal at Winston, 1895; Salisbury State Normal at Salisbury, 1896; Goldsboro Normal at Goldsboro, 1886; Franklinton Normal at Franklinton, 1881; and Elizabeth City State Normal at Elizabeth City, 1897.[35] Of these seven state normal schools, only three are in existence today —Fayetteville, Winston-Salem, and Elizabeth City—and they have developed into well established four-year teachers' colleges.

Graded Schools

Following the establishing of the normal schools, came the graded schools. These so-called graded schools provided classification of children according to their ages and attainments and usually required a teacher for each grade. They did not provide for either the exceptional or for the slow learner. A child could not take a subject in a higher or a lower grade than the one in which he was classified. The earliest graded schools were the result of local initiative aided by the Peabody Fund. The charters for some of the cities provided for the setting up of graded schools.

---

32. Robert Bingham, *op. cit.*, p. 21.

33. Charles William Dabney, *Universal Education in the South*, Vol. I. pp. 116, 117.

34. Hugh Lefler and Albert Newsome, *op. cit.*, p. 501.

35. Superintendents' Correspondence, Miscellaneous Negro Schools, 1867, 1907 State Department Archives.

The first graded school for whites was established in Greensboro in 1870 and soon thereafter a similar one was opened for Negroes. Charlotte, with the aid of the Peabody Fund established a graded school in 1873 for whites, but because of a contest in court, the graded schools in Charlotte were not opened until 1882.

Alexander Graham, Superintendent of Schools in Fayetteville in 1878, is said to have been "the father of the graded schools in North Carolina." The beginning of the graded schools came about as a result of a court trial during which six Negro boys who had been taught in a school supported by northern philanthropy were able to sign their names to their testimony, while five white boys who had attended only an eight weeks' public school could not sign their names. Whereupon, the whites, with the aid of the Peabody Fund, decided to open a graded school for white children in 1878.[36]

The Goldsboro Graded Schools were established in 1881. Said the late Judge Frank Daniels, brother of Josephus Daniels:

> The first vote I ever cast was for the establishment of the Goldsboro Graded Schools. When I came in 1881 to the Goldsboro Bar, we had nothing of much worth but private schools and it was a great fight whether the Government would take over the function of training its future citizens. The fight was won and the graded school (sic) was formed. [37]

Reports to State Superintendent S. M. Finger for the year ending May 28, 1886, include the following interesting information: Superintendent of the Goldsboro Graded Schools, Edwin A. Alderman; average salary of teachers, not including the superintendent, $39; number of grades, 9; number of teachers, 13; enrollment, 550; tuition, free; State appropriation, $1,000; value of property, $22,000. The report does not show any figures relative to the status of colored schools in Goldsboro.

A tabulation of Superintendent Finger's reports from several cities which had graded schools in 1885, follows:

---

36. Charles William Dabney, *op. cit.,* pp. 189, 190.

37. Frank A. Daniels, Address, *Dedication of Wayne County Court House, November 30, 1914, History of Wayne County,* p. 37.

	Race	No. of Grades	Enroll-ment	Months Taught	Tuition	State Approp.	Salary	Value of Property
Washington	W	6	200	2	$1.20	$1,940.00	$45	$1,500
	C	6	400	2	.95	3,308.00	45	55
Salisbury	W	8	357	9	1.23	996.00	45	6,000
	C	None Reported						
Raleigh	W	7	751	8	9.00	2,260.00	53	25,500
	C	5	1274	8	7.50	2,810.00	40	9,000
Goldsboro	W	9	550	10	Free	1,000.00	39	22,000
	C	None Reported						
Wilson	W	8	401	10	11.05	750.55	41	950
	C	None Reported						
Magnolia	W	3	105	5	.87	80.00	55	Nothing
	C	5	80	4	None	80.00	45	55
New Bern	W	11	515	10	10.00	600.00	35	2,500
	C	None Reported						
Greensboro	W	10	300	10	10.00	218.00	30	6,000
	C	10	100	10			30	
Charlotte	W	9	805	9		1,789.00	39	18,000
	C	9	700	9		1,920.00	27	2,000

The report from which this tabulation comes states that in Mitchell County there were no schools for either race.[38]

38. F. M. Finger, Superintendents' Correspondence 1880-1886; State Department Archives.

Church Schools

It would be impossible to tell the story of all the church and private schools which were established during Reconstruction and Recovery, but a broad sampling of these institutions will give the contemporary student of education some appreciation of the struggles of the patriarchs of our educational heritage. Those institutions of higher education, existing in 1958-59, will be discussed in a later chapter.

The Neuse River Baptist Association, organized at Halifax in 1866, made a feeble effort to establish a school at Weldon. A site was purchased with a small building and for two years a school was operated until the building burned. A new site outside of Weldon was purchased for the continuation of the school.[39]

To organize and maintain schools, the Baptists, with encouragement of the Home Mission Society, formed associations over the state. These associations often conflicted and the greatest hindrance to their schools came from ministers, themselves. Superstition and strife were rampant and much opposition against the establishment of schools existed.

Shiloh Institute

Established at Warrenton in 1885, Shiloh Institute was credited with sending out one hundred twenty-five teachers and several ministers within the twelve years of its existence.

Garysburg High School had been established by the Reverend R. I. Walden prior to the establishment of Shiloh.[40]

Waters Normal Institute

Founded in 1886 at Winton, Waters Institute was one of the ablest schools in the state. Because of the efficiency of the school, it received a larger appropriation from the Home Mission Society than any other school aided by the society. C. S. Brown, its principal, was a man of rare gifts and was interested in almost everything which meant the uplift of his people. He influenced many families to move to Winton and to build beautiful homes.[41] The school still exists but as a part of the public school system.

Albion Academy

Albion Academy was established by the Presbyterian Church in 1878 at Franklinton. Its first principal was the Reverend Moses Hopkins. Its purpose was to train teachers. In 1881, it was chartered as a State Normal School and remained so until 1903, when

---

39. J. A. Whitted, *op. cit.*, pp. 79, 80.

40. *Ibid.*, p. 166.

41. *Ibid.*, p. 169.

the state normal schools were consolidated. It then reverted to the original sponsorship, the Presbyterian Church and under the principalship of the Reverend J. A. Savage.[42] In 1933, Albion was merged with Red Stone Academy of Lumberton and Mary Potter School at Oxford.

Thompson Institute

Thompson Institute was established in 1881 at Lumberton under the auspices of the Lumber River Baptist Association and was named for the oldest minister of the association, the Reverend A. H. Thompson. At the time of the setting up of this institution, there was not a good dwelling belonging to a Negro Baptist anywhere in the section of Lumberton. By 1900, a poor dwelling was an exception. D. J. Avery was the first principal of the school. He was succeeded by W. H. Knuckles, who greatly improved the school's physical facilities. In 1905 most of the teachers in the surrounding territory were products of Thompson Institute. A small appropriation was received from the Baptist Home Mission Society of New York, but its main support came from the Lumber River Association, of which the Reverend J. D. Harrell was for many years the moderator.[43]

Goldsboro Normal and Classical Institute

This institution was established under the auspices of the Friends Freedmen's Association September, 1886, with Miss Louise S. Dorr, a white teacher, who for 13 years had presided over the Johnson Normal School in Raleigh. The school was to run for a term of nine months.

J. A. Bonitz, Chairman of the Board of Education and Editor of the Goldsboro Messenger, endorsed the school in the following words:

> It affords me pleasure to give my earnest endorsement to the projected Normal and Classical Institute for the education of colored teachers and I trust the laudable efforts of our colored citizens may enlist the sympathy and substantial effort of philanthropic citizens at home and elsewhere. I am quite sure that it will not be abused by those who have the management of the institution in their keeping.

The school was also endorsed by E. O. Wright, Superintendent of Wayne County. With the consolidation of the state normal schools in 1903, the Goldsboro Normal was abolished.[44]

---

42. Superintendents' Correspondence, 1867-1907, Miscellaneous Negro Schools.

43. J. A. Whitted, op. cit., p. 178.

44. Superintendents' Correspondence, 1867-1909 (Miscellaneous Negro Schools) State Department Archives.

Mary Potter School

Through the efforts of the Reverend George Clayton Shaw and the interest of Mrs. Mary Potter, Secretary of the Freedmen's Board in the Albany, New York Presbyterial Synodical, a parochial school was started at Oxford, September, 1889. In 1892, the school was named "Mary Potter" in honor of the friend whose influence led the Albany Presbyterial societies to contribute toward its effort. Under the wise and efficient leadership of Dr. Shaw, Mary Potter became one of the best secondary schools of the state. In 1933, the school was merged with Albion Academy of Franklinton, and Red Stone Academy of Lumberton and the Reverend H. S. Davis became the principal.[45] The school has continued as an accredited high school under the public school system.

Roanoke Normal and Industrial-Theological Institute.

This institution was established in 1896 at Eliabeth City by the Roanoke Baptist Missionary Association under the leadership of I. B. Roach. Its first principal was Dr. M. W. D. Norman, Dean of the Theological Department of Shaw University.[46] It continued as a secondary school under the Reverend C. F. Graves until recent years when its functions have been largely the training of ministers.

Henderson Institute

This institution was founded in 1890 at Henderson under the auspices of the Freedmen's Board of the United Presbyterian Church.[47] It continued for many years under the able leadership of Dr. J. A. Cotton and is now a part of the public school system.

New Bern Collegiate and Industrial

This institution was set up at New Bern in 1902 as an independent private school by the Reverend A. L. E. Weeks, a minister of the Baptist Church. The school received a small contribution from the Home Mission Society, but was largely maintained through the energies of the Reverend Mister Weeks and by local white and colored friends. The school no longer exists, but

> Much light was diffused and much good accomplished through this one man showing that "Where there's a will, there's a way."[48]

Gregory Institute

This school was set up under the auspices of the American Mis-

---

45. Rowena Hunter Davis, *A History of Mary Potter School*, Unpublished Thesis, North Carolina College, 1944, p. 30.

46. W. N. Hartshorne, *op. cit.*, p. 361.

47. W. N. Hartshorne, *op. cit.*, p. 216.

48. J. A. Whitted, *op. cit.*, pp. 180, 182.

sionary Association, April 3, 1865, at Wilmington and was one of the first of the so-called A.M.A. Schools established in North Carolina. Its first building was erected from funds given by a Mr. Williston of Massachusetts in 1868. It was originally known as Wilmington Normal; later as New Hampshire Memorial Institute. In 1881, the Honorable J. N. Gregory, of Massachusetts, erected a brick church, a teachers' home, and enlarged the school building, which became Gregory Institute.[49]

Peabody Academy

This school, also one of the American Missionary Association projects, was set up in 1880 at Troy and for many years was headed by the Reverend O. Faduma, a native African.[50]

Lincoln Academy.

The school, another of the American Missionary Association institutions, was established in 1892 for the training of girls in the art of homemaking and for the training of teachers and ministers.[51]

Joseph K. Brick School

This school was founded under the auspices of the American Missionary Association by T. S. Inborden at Bricks, near Enfield. In the heart of the peanut section, this institution had a great influence upon the farmers of the section aside from exerting a wholesome educational service in the training of teachers.[52] About 1924, it became a junior college and later dropped its junior college status to become a standard high school under the public school system. The institution is now being operated under the name of "Franklinton Center" for the promotion of farm and home life activities.

Saint Michael's Church and Industrial School

St. Michael's School was founded at Charlotte in 1882 by the Reverend P. R. Alston and under the auspices of the Protestant Episcopal Church.[53]

Billingsley Memorial Academy

Billingsley was established in 1889 at Statesville by S. F. Wentz

---

49. W. N. Hartshorne, *op. cit.*, p. 160.

50. *Ibid.*, p. 159.

51. *Ibid.*, p. 157.

52. *Ibid.*, p. 147.

53. *Ibid.*, p. 257.

under the auspices of the Presbyterian Board of Missions for Freedmen.[54]

Eastern Academy

The school was founded in 1895 at New Bern under the auspices of the African Methodist Episcopal Zion Church. Its chief object was to train ministers.[55] However, many teachers of the New Bern area received their training at this institution.

Thus we have attempted to recognize contributions of most of the religious denominations in various sections of the state. As indicated before, it is not possible to record every contribution and effort to establish and to maintain schools by all the associations and private individuals, but it is an effort to show the great interest and ambitions of the times among those who laid the foundation for the enlightenment of the Negro in North Carolina.

Summary

The Period of Reconstruction and Recovery was one of great stress and strain for the people of North Carolina and indeed for the entire South. The spirit was willing, but the flesh was weak. At the beginning of Reconstruction, the situation among whites was one of hopelessness; that among the Negroes was more hopeful. The South had lost nearly everything; the Negroes had had nothing to lose. Besides, northern philanthropy had already begun operating schools for Negroes; while most white schools had closed. Yet the progress of the education of the Negroes was inextricably involved with the status of the whites among whom the Negroes had to live.

The great needs of the time were: a real spirit and determination to rise from the ruins of the war; adequate funds to operate a system of education; and trained teachers to instruct the children. Some effort, though feeble, was made by the legislature to provide tax money to support schools, but there was little money to be had.

Fortunately and strangely enough, financial aid came from an unexpected source, the Peabody Fund, established by a northern philanthropist.

While only the well established schools were the main recipients of the Peabody money, it encouraged others to meet its conditions and went far toward influencing the establishing of normal schools and graded schools.

The establishing of state normal schools increased the supply of trained teachers and the organization of graded schools boosted the work of the normal schools.

Missionary associations and church associations set up schools in every section of the state to provide elementary and secondary

---

54. *Ibid.*, p. 213.

55. *Ibid.*, p. 295.

education for Negro children. Shaw University in Raleigh and Biddle University in Charlotte were in the vanguard for the training of teachers for the various missionary and church schools.

Despite the acute problems of the times, the Period of Reconstruction and Recovery gave birth to many great educators of both races, many of whom are identified with the great new birth known as "Universal Education," which the next chapter will treat and reverently call the "Era of Aycock."

Chapter IV

Era Of Aycock

The chapter is called the Era of Aycock because Charles Brantley Aycock was the culminating spirit of the developments in Negro Education of the period. However, the chapter includes phases of that development which existed before and after his time as well as phases not exclusively appertaining to Negroes. It includes much of the functions of educational funds and boards which had so much to do with education of both races and laid the foundation for a later period of secondary educational development which will portray the work of N. C. Newbold.

The early part of this era, the last decade of the 19th Century, was fraught with political maneuverings which had a tremendous impact upon the status of education. It was the period of Fusion politics when the Negro question seemed to be the "fly in the ointment," and had come to be associated with the Populist-Republican administration.[1]

The Platform of the Peoples' Party in 1898 would broaden Public School System as rapidly as proper regard for the taxpayers' interest and resources permit; and also favor such revision of our present school system as may increase the efficiency and insure the most competent and effective supervision.[2]

Under the leadership of Charles H. Mebane, State Superintendent of Public Instruction, the Fusionists restored the office of County Superintendent and every school district was required to vote on the issue of local school taxes every two years until the taxes were approved. A legislative appropriation of $50,000 was made to aid the schools in those districts which voted for local school taxes.[3]

While politicians were clamoring for a division of the tax funds by race, statesmen like Charles D. McIver and Edwin A. Alderman were advocating universal education as the real solution of the State's big problem. By 1897 education in North Carolina began to enjoy a new birth. Mebane succeeded in soliciting the aid of the newspapers rather than the politicians. As a result the legislature of 1897 enacted a new law providing local taxation as a basis of public school support with a state appropriation in an equal amount not to exceed $500. The proposal, however, was defeated,[4] at least for the time being as we shall see with the ascendency of Charles B. Aycock.

1. Hugh Talmage Lefler, *North Carolina History.*

2. "The North Carolinian," May 18, 1898.

3. Lefler and Newsome, *North Carolina*, p. 519.

4. J. G. De Roulhac Hamilton, *History of North Carolina*, Vol. III, pp. 364-366.

Universal Education

Although universal education is closely identified with Aycock, it had its beginning long before the great "Educational Governor" rose to state and national prominence. However, politics and the question of the status of the Negro militated against any consolidated effort which might have had tangible results in building an adequate school system for the state.

While politics raged and racial animosities mounted, Southern statesmanship and Northern philanthropy were sowing seeds of public confidence calculated to reap a far more profitable educational harvest than the politicians could have possibly guaranteed.

While Northern philanthropy played an important role in the education of the Negro, it was Southern evangelism that was more far reaching in the permanent progress of universal education in the South.

Oddly enough in North Carolina the leader in the great movement was a man named Moses; Edward Pearson Moses, Superintendent of Schools in Goldsboro, who did pioneer work in organizing schools for both races in Goldsboro. While conducting summer schools at the University he met Edwin A. Alderman, James Y. Joyner, P. P. Claxton, and Charles D. McIver all of whom had planned to study law, but were influenced by Moses to change their objective to education.

Moses is credited with having trained these young men and fired them with enthusiasm. They all became great teachers and leaders in the campaigns for universal education.

P. P. Claxton, who at one time was Superintendent of Schools in Goldsboro and later United States Commissioner of Education, said of Moses:

> I feel quite sure that Alderman, McIver, and I, and the other men of our ages, including J. Y. Joyner and D. B. Johnson, owed our inspiration and our zeal for the causes of public education almost wholly to Moses. . . . Moses was a modern Pestalozzi, the most enthusiastic and inspiring man I have ever known. His voice was that of one crying in the wilderness, and was heard by a few at first, and then by more and more until it became a popular chorus on the highways.[5]

Philanthropy—(Slater Fund)

The first of the great Northern funds aiding education in the South was the Peabody Fund, which was discussed in Chapter III. Another great fund, devoted exclusively to Negro schools, is known as the Slater Fund.

In 1882, John F. Slater, of Norwich, Connecticut, gave one mil-

---

5. Charles William Dabney, *Universal Education in the South*, Vol. I, pp. 194-195.

lion dollars to establish a fund exclusively for the education of the Negro in Southern states. The objective of this fund was

The uplifting of the lately emancipated populations of the Southern states and their posterity, by conferring upon them the blessings of Christian education, such as shall tend to make them good men and good citizens.

As in the case of the Peabody Fund, a college president, Dr. Atticud G. Haygood, President of Emory University, resigned his presidency to direct the fund.

The immediate object of the fund was "For instituting trades and other manual occupations." Dr. Haygood's book, "Our Brother In Black," was an appeal for cooperation of southern whites in behalf of Negroes. When he resigned to become a Bishop, he was succeeded by another devoted southerner, Dr. J. L. M. Curry, under whose guidance, the spirit of cooperation between North and South was fostered to an even larger growth.

The six provisions under which schools could secure aid from the Slater Fund were as follows:

1. Practical education in books and always under Christian influence

2. Not to establish new schools, but make more efficient such as were or might be established by others

3. To select for aid those schools that did the best work in preparing men and women to teach the children of their own race

4. To help as many schools as the proceeds allowed, so as not to make appropriations inefficient

5. So to use it as to make it a diffusive stimulant to the Negroes themselves and to other friends who might help them

6. To prefer those schools that recognize and introduce industrial training.[6]

Later functions of the Slater Fund will be discussed in connection with the County Training School movement. Between the years 1882 and 1930 Negro institutions in North Carolina received a total of $331,165 from the Slater Fund.[7]

The Southern Education Board

Before the close of the Century many educational statesmen, North as well as South, began a movement destined to change the attitude of many opposed to public education in general and to the education of the Negro in particular. The movement originated from a series of conferences suggested by an Episcopal minister, Dr. Edward Abbott, of New York, during the summer of 1898.

Dr. Abbott proposed to Captain William H. Sale, a hotel pro-

---

6. W. N. Hartshorne, *Era of Progress and Promise*, p. 543.

7. Division of Negro Education 1914-38, State Archives, Raleigh.

prietor at Capon Springs, West Virginia, that an invitation be extended to educators for a conference on the advancement of education. This conference met June 29, 1898. It included such men as Bishop Thomas Dudley of Kentucky, Dr. H. B. Frissell of Hampton Institute, Dr. A. B. Hunter of Saint Augustine's College of Raleigh, Dr. Julius D. Drecher of Roanoke College, and others. The conference considered such topics as: How far can the public school system in the South be improved and made effective? and How far is it feasible to introduce industrial education? Twelve states and the District of Columbia were represented. Altogether thirty-six persons of both races were in attendance. It continued in session from June 29 to July 2 and effected a permanent organization, changed from "Conference on Christian Education" to "Conference for Education in the South."

The second conference at Capon Springs in June, 1899, was dedicated to universal education in the South. An important addition to the personnel of the conference was that of Robert C. Ogden of New York, who brought in his private car some distinguished Northern guests, the first of a series of excursions into the South, organized and conducted by Ogden, which Walter Hines Page called "excursions into enobling experiences."

The third conference met at Capon Springs June 27, 1900. As the first two conferences had been concerned mostly with Negro education, the third was to give attention to the neglected education of whites as the best way to provide training for the Negroes.

The educational problem of the South was one problem, not two, and could not be treated by separate measures. Separate schools there must be, but these schools would have to be provided in one body of laws and the system supported by taxes by all the people. As the whites must inevitably pay the greater part of these taxes, they must first be convinced that the only way to make good and useful citizens of the Negroes was through proper training in the schools.

The discussions therefore considered the needs of education of both races.

A fourth conference, held at Winston-Salem April 18-20, 1901 brought John D. Rockefeller, Jr., as one of Ogden's guests, and Charles B. Aycock, Governor of the State. This conference was a culmination of the activities of the first three in that it became an exponent for Universal Education and brought about the birth of the Southern Education Board, which in turn gave rise to the General Education Board.

From the conference in Winston-Salem, the Committee on Southern Education was made up as follows: Honorable J. L. M. Curry, Dr. C. W. Dabney, Dr. Edwin A. Alderman, Dr. Charles D. McIver, Dr H. B. Frissell, George Foster Peabody, Rev. Wallace Buttrick, and Robert C. Ogden, Chairman.

After a series of conferences in New York, Bar Harbor, Maine, and in Asheville, N. C., the Committee met November 4, 1901 and organized "The Southern Education Board" with Robert C. Ogden, president, Charles D. McIver, secretary, and George Foster Peabody, treasurer. The first function of the Southern Education Board was for the creation of public opinion for schools. The second was to set up a Board of Trustees to handle gifts from private persons, boards, and foundations to promote public education.

This board of Trustees became the General Education Board which handled all financial operations while the Southern Education Board devoted itself to the work of creating public opinion in behalf of the public schools. Among the objectives agreed upon were voluntary local taxation for better schools, compulsory education, longer terms, consolidation of weak schools, and industrial and agricultural education.[8]

General Education Board

Rockefeller contributed $53,000,000 in a series of large gifts between 1902 and 1909 to be disbursed by the General Education Board toward the needs of Southern Education. Dabney and Claxton, through their Bureau of Investigation and Information, secured the active participation of newspapers all over the South. Aside from these media they sent out thousands of bulletins and circular letters, reports, and documents to be used among the various states for the campaign of Universal Education.

Although North Carolina had already begun her campaign for Universal Education, the Southern Education Board doubtless gave great impetus to the movement. (See Aycock and Negro Disfranchisement). Between 1900 and 1913, North Carolina's expenditures for education rose from $950,317 to $4,067,793.[9]

Aside from its interest in formal education in the schools, one of the greatest contributions of the General Education Board was its efforts toward improving the farmers' plight. This was done by persuading the farmers to adopt new and efficient methods of cultivation and thus improve productivity. The Board discovered Seaman A. Knapp, later dubbed "Apostle of the Cow Pea," who went straight to the dirt farmer to conduct on his own land a demonstration of new methods. This was the beginning of the farm demonstration work in the South.[10]

The story now shifts from philanthropy to the main subject of the chapter, Charles Brantley Aycock. In order to understand and appreciate the role of Aycock, it is necessary to know something of the Negroes' role in the politics of the period.

---

8. Dabney, Vol II, *Op. cit.*, pp. 5-59 and C. Vann Woodward, *Origins of The New South*, 1951, pp. 402-403.

9. *Ibid.*, p. 405-406.

10. *Ibid.*, p. 408-410.

Aycock and Negro Disfranchisement.

As indicated earlier, Negroes had been ushered into politics during the Period of Reconstruction and had increased their political
activity under the Fusion Rule of the Nineties. The holding of
political office by Negroes was distasteful to whites. Besides the
Negro in politics was embarrassing to the Populists and white Re-
publicans while the Democrats disliked him because he was almost
exclusively Republican. The chief criticism of the Democrats was
"Negro domination." Dignified politicians described the situation
as a lack of good government.

However, Negroes did not dominate government at any time as
they constituted not more than one fifth of the total membership
of the General Assembly and only four Negroes had served a total
of fourteen years in Congress; J. A. Hyman (1875-77), J. E. O'Hara
(1883-87), H. P. Cheatham (1889-93) and George N. White (1897-
1901). Of the four, only Hyman had not attended college and only
O'Hara was a carpet bagger.[11]

During the fusion period of the nineties, there were ten Negroes
elected to the state legislature, four were elected aldermen in Wilmington, two in New Bern, two in Greenville, one or two in Raleigh,
county treasurer and a coroner in New Hanover County and minor
positions here and there.[12]

In some of the eastern counties of the state Negroes, outnumber-
ing the whites, were largely in control of much of the local government and held federal positions as well. This situation engendered
serious racial conflict and influenced the organization of the "Red
Shirts," dedicated to the overthrow of Negro domination. It cul-
minated in the tragic Wilmington Riot when violence superseded
reason. "White supremacy," a term obnoxious to Negroes, became
the battle cry of its proponents.[13]

All the southern states by one means or another passed laws to
disfranchise the Negro and thus to neutralize his influence and
practice in government and politics.

In North Carolina it took the form of an educational suffrage
amendment, which contained the famous "grandfather clause."
The amendment provided educational requirements (ability to
read and write) and poll tax payments as a requisite for voting, but
excepted all persons who were entitled to vote in any state on or
before January 1, 1867 and their lineal descendants; provided that
all such persons registered in accordance with the requirements of
the constitution prior to December 1, 1908.[14]

Aycock campaigned upon the basis of this proposed amendment

---

11. Lefler and Newsome, *North Carolina*, p. 518.

12. Helen Edmunds, *The Negro and Fusion Politics*, p. 219.

13. Hugh T. Lefler, *Op. cit.*, pp. 397, 399.

14. Conner and Poe, *The Life and Speeches of Charles B. Aycock*, p. 73.

which was overwhelmingly adopted and Aycock was elected Governor in 1900.

Understanding Aycock.

In order to appreciate fully the contribution of Aycock to universal education in general and to the education of the Negro in particular, it is important to understand the inherent philosophy of the man. In the first place, he is bound to have inherited the natural sentiments of his forebears with respect to loyalty to the state and to Southern traditions. During the Civil War his father was in the state Senate and supported the Confederate prosecution of the war.

Secondly, Aycock was a politician and, as such, would utilize any expedient as a means to an end until elected and then act as he believed in the best interest of all the people.

In the third place, Aycock had a profound conviction that good government for North Carolina rested upon the assured political supremacy of the white race.[15]

Finally, it is important to understand the political status of the Negro at the time of the ascendancy of Aycock. As already indicated, many Negroes were holding political office; federal, state, and local. Aside from this fact, there were upwards of 125,000 Negro voters with no restriction whatever upon their participation in elections. They actually constituted a balance of power and practically all were identified with the Republican Party.[16]

Aycock's Campaign.

While Aycck campaigned for the white supremacy amendment, at the same time he just as aggressively advocated "Universal Education." He pledged the people that there would be schools for all if he were elected. In many of his campaign tours, he had more interested audiences of educational interest than of political. His listeners were college professors, ministers, doctors, business men and citizens in general.[17]

Said Aycock:
> If you vote for me, I want you to do so with the distinct understanding that I shall devote the four years of my official term to the upbuilding of the public schools of North Carolina. I shall endeavor for every child in the State to get an education.[18]

Aycock—Educational Governor.

In his inaugural address, Aycock renewed his pledge on educa-

---

15. *Ibid.*, p. 61.
16. *Ibid.*, p. 69.
17. Dabney, Vol. II, *Op. cit.*, p. 96.
18. Conner and Poe, *Op. cit.*, p. 85.

cation and general improvement of the public school system.

On a hundred platforms, to half the voters of the State ... I pledged the State its strength, its heart, its wealth to universal education. . . . For my part I declare to you that it shall be my constant aim and effort during the four years that I shall endeavor to serve the people of this State to redeem this most solemn of all our pledges.[19]

Aycock gave greater impetus to universal education in the South than any other man. As he was the leader of North Carolina so was North Carolina leader of the South. He was known and sought as a speaker from Maine to Georgia, and Oklahoma. His whole creed was for educating everybody and educating everything.

Though rising upon the issue of disfranchisement of the Negro, he actually was a friend to the Negro. When an amendment to divide the tax funds on the basis of what each race paid, Aycock threatened to resign if it were adopted. He would regard the adoption of such an amendment as a violation of his pledge to the people and of the plighted faith of his party.[20]

During the Aycock era, the percentage of illiteracy among Negroes decreased from 47.6 to 31.9; public sentiment for schools increased, and the foundation for modern rural and urban secondary education was laid.

Aycock continued his advocacy of Universal Education following his retirement from the governorship and died while making an educational address at Birmingham, Alabama, April 4, 1912.

Summary.

The core of the Chapter is "Universal Education" which had its inception in the activities of men like Edward Preston Moses and was enhanced by men like Alderman, Claxton, and McIver.

The Slater Fund, the Southern Education and the General Education Boards gave great impetus to the educational needs and the union of efforts to create public sentiment for universal education.

The increasing activities of the Negro in politics and government caused the rise of white supremacy which resulted in disfranchisement and the ascendancy of Charles B. Aycock to the governorship. Aycock's pledge for public schools for all and his fight for universal education made North Carolina the leading state of the South and earned for him the enobling title of "Educational Governor."

---

19. *Ibid.*, pp. 117-118.

20. Dabney, Vol. II, p. 345 and Conner and Poe, *Op. cit.*, pp. 133-134.

Chapter V

The Era Of Newbold

This chapter will endeavor to focus attention upon a personality unique in the education of Negroes in North Carolina. He was N. C. Newbold, whom some friends dubbed "North Carolina" Newbold, so thoroughly was he interested in, informed about, and active for more than a quarter of a century in the complete education of Negroes in North Carolina.

If Aycock was the apostle of universal education, Newbold was the embodiment of Negro education, for he truly dedicated his life to the promotion of every phase of the education of colored people. As state agent he steered the activities of the Jeanes Rural School Program; under the Slater Board he set up the county training school system and organized the garden clubs which developed into the Home Demonstration service; as Director of The Division of Negro Education, he set in motion the development and standardization of secondary schools; and through his direction the normal schools became four-year teachers' colleges.

His influence extended even beyond the bounds of North Carolina, for annually he would convoke large conferences, sometimes in the state, other times out of the state, at which were gathered educators of both races in the South—church men, state officials, and plain businessmen to whom he preached the gospel of Negro Education.

This chapter will be devoted to the contributions of the Jeanes Fund, the Phelps-Stokes Fund, the County Training School movement, the Rosenwald Schools, and the development of the modern high schools, all of which are identified with the work of N. C. Newbold.

The growth and development of the normal schools, now teachers' colleges, and that of the other colleges of the State will be the subject of a later chapter. Suffice it to say, Newbold was the controlling influence in all this development, which rightly entitles his name to be the subject of the chapter, "The Era of Newbold."

The Jeanes Fund.

"Lest we forget" and overlook the contributing influences of the white people of the South, the name of J. L. M. Curry must be mentioned. Jabez Lamar Monroe Curry was born in Georgia and served in the Confederate Congress and also in the Confederate army. Studying law at Harvard University broadened his interest in public affairs. He embraced every opportunity to hear such men as Daniel Webster, Henry Barnard, and Horace Mann. From Mann came much of the enthusiasm which later influenced his activities toward Universal education.[1]

As agent for the Peabody Fund, succeeding Dr. Barnas Sears, Curry appeared before city councils, county courts, and state legislatures, and committees of Congress, pleading with eloquence and effect the cause of the public schools. His example and enthusiasm inspired others to work for the same cause and by 1900 their efforts were beginning to bear fruit. We have observed that fact in the story of the Peabody Fund, the Slater Fund, and the establishing of the Southern and General Education Boards.

In line with the same tradition of philosophy was the establishing of the Jeanes Fund in 1907. At the time of this writing, 1959, the Jeanes Fund was still in existence, supplementing funds for the promotion of rural supervision of Negro schools.

What is the Jeanes Fund and how did it arise? Despite the disfranchisement period when Negroes saw their political freedom virtually abolished; when lynching had reached an unprecedented total of 155 in a single year; and when illiteracy had become a challenge to advocates of white supremacy, the South still had many men with larger hearts, wider vision, and deeper sense of justice. Such men as Aycock in North Carolina, George Foster Peabody in Georgia, and Edgar Gardner Murphy of Alabama realized the fact that education for all was the real answer to the challenges of the times.

It was during times like these when men and women in the Southern states were becoming increasingly conscious both of the great need of their people and of new opportunities for service that the Jeanes Fund began its work[2]

Miss Anna T. Jeanes, a Quaker lady of great affluence in Philadelphia, was first induced by George Foster Peabody in 1905 to make a contribution to Negro education. She contributed $200,000 "for the assistance of Negro Rural Schools" to be expended under the direction of Hampton and Tuskegee. In 1906 she contributed another donation, $10,000 for Hampton and the same for Tuskegee. At the same time she said, "I should like to help the little country schools for Negroes." To this cause she gave $1,000,000.[3]

Thus in 1907 was born the Jeanes Fund for the promotion of supervision of the Negro rural schools in the South.

It is difficult to estimate the far reaching importance of the Jeanes Fund work, for it encompassed the lives of so many thousands of individuals—men, women and children—who came under the benign influence of the Jeanes teacher. She lived in their homes, she worshipped in their churches, she worked in their parent-teacher meetings; in a word, she was like "one of the fam-

---

1. Dabney, Charles William, *Universal Education in the South*, Vol. I pp. 123, 124.

2. Jones, Lance G. E., *The Jeanes Teacher in the United States, 1908-33*, pp. 3, 5.

3. Dabney, Universal Education, Vol. II, p. 445.

ily" among most of the households in the various communities of her county.

The writer was intimately and actively associated with Jeanes teachers (they later came to be called Jeanes supervisors) for more than forty years and can truthfully state that they were among the most devoted group of educators it has been his opportunity to know.

At the outset the Jeanes teacher was sent out to foster industrial or home-making functions among the rural schools. She would be found teaching and supervising domestic science and domestic art among the girls and chair caning, mat making, and wood working among the boys.

State Superintendent J. Y. Joyner sent out the following memoranda in 1913 to clarify the relationship of Mr. N. C. Newbold with the Jeanes teachers and also to outline the functions of the Jeanes teachers' work.

> The title of Mr. Newbold is Associate Supervisor of Rural Elementary Schools. He will reach the counties through the county superintendent and the county supervisors.

At this time, 1913-14, there were 16 counties of the state in which the industrial teachers (Jeanes supervisors) were at work. These supervisors were paid wholly or in part by the Jeanes Fund.

Continuing the memoranda, Superintendent Joyner described their duties as follows:

> To visit the colored schools in the county one or more times in the school year
>
> To help encourage the local teachers to teach sanitation, serving, cooking, basket making, chair caning, mat making
>
> To help the boys in simple carpentry, making axe helves, hoe handles, mending broken farm tools, how to handle tools
>
> To encourage better sanitary conditions in homes and schools
>
> To meet men and women in the district and form Improvement Leagues or Betterment Associations, the object of which is to better the living conditions among colored people
>
> To paint or whitewash houses
>
> To raise money for better schools and to extend terms
>
> To encourage home and school gardens, tomato clubs, corn clubs
>
> To promote higher standards of living, integrity, honesty, and thrift.

Mr. Newbold was directed to secure cooperation of all higher institutions in organizing and promoting courses in industrial education to provide for training of Jeanes industrial teachers.[4]

---

4. Newbold, N. C., *Correspondence, Division of Negro Education*, State Department Archives.

As the Jeanes teacher was usually an outstandng personality, superintendents began to rely more and more upon their worth and integrity; so that, in nearly every situation, the Jeanes supervisors virtually served as assistants to the county superintendents and exercised great influence in the selection of teachers and in the development of the educational program of their counties.

After the establishment of the Negro Division of Education, with Newbold as Director, a state supervisor of the Jeanes program was appointed. The first state supervisor of this sort was Mrs. Annie W. Holland, whose life and work will appear in a later chapter.

From a report of Mrs. Holland to Mr. Newbold in 1932 we find the following outline of the Jeanes Supervisor's program, which shows how far-reaching the work had developed from its early objectives:

Outline of Work

To improve the quality of instruction County and Group Meetings: Reading Circle, Study group, Extension course, summer school

Conferences	Libraries
Promotions	Industrial arts
Visitation	Field work
Follow-up	Standard Tests
Health Program	Office Work
Community Cooperation[5]	

From Mr. Newbold's own report on activities and expenditures of the Jeanes Fund in 1928-29 we note as follows:

Beginning in 1908, the Jeanes Fund has contributed about $172,325 to salaries of Jeanes Teachers in North Carolina. The work has been spread over the state and today (1929) we have 39 Jeanes teachers in 41 counties. Jeanes teachers in 1927-28 raised $41,121.29 and up to February 1929, $14,171.46 for improving rural education.

The business of these traveling teachers, working under the direction of the county superintendent, is to help and encourage the rural teacher to introduce into small country schools simple home industries, to give talks and lessons on sanitation, cleanliness and to promote the improvement of school houses and grounds and to organize clubs for the betterment of the school and neighborhood.[6]

Again, "lest we forget," or in case we have never known, the name of another great southern benefactor, James Hardy Dillard must be mentioned.

Born in Virginia, he attended Washington College (now Washington and Lee University) in Lexington, Virginia, and became a

---

5. *Ibid.*, 1913-14.

6. *Ibid.*, 1913-14.

classical scholar. Teaching in New Orleans, he became a trustee of four Negro colleges. One of them, Dillard University in New Orleans, is named for him.

In 1908, he accepted the directorship of the Jeanes Rural Fund and in 1910, he took up where J. L. M. Curry left off, the directorship of the Slater Fund. He was also a member of the Southern Education Board, and of the General Education Board and became vice president of the Phelps-Stokes Fund. He was a great favorite of Negro educators from the smallest of rural institutions to the greatest of the colleges. He held the directorship of the Jeanes Fund until 1931.[7]

Although two other directors followed Dr. Dillard, the history of the Jeanes Fund is largely the story of the work of James Hardy Dillard. At the time of his passing the Jeanes Fund had almost outlived its usefulness; at least public education had assumed most of its responsibility in the rural as well as urban school systems.

However, the Jeanes Fund is still in operation (1959) though, like all the other great funds, it is a part of the Southern Education Foundation, Incorporated, which absorbed the residue of the Peabody, the John F. Slater, and the Virginia Randolph Funds on July 1, 1937.[8]

Although many outstanding women and a few men were Jeanes supervisors only a few early ones are mentioned here: Mary A. Charlton-Holliday, of Columbus County and later of Iredell County; Annie W. Holland, of Gates; later to become the first State Supervisor of Elementary Schools; and Marie McIver, of Halifax; later a State Supervisor. Outstanding men who served as Jeanes Supervisors included T. T. Ringer, of Duplin, G. R. Whitfield, of Pitt, and J. R. Faison, of Anson counties.

The Phelps-Stokes Fund

Caroline Phelps Stokes was interested in the education of the Negro from childhood. Upon her death in 1909 she willed a great sum to be devoted to education of Negroes both in Africa and in the United States.

The work of the fund was to consist of investigations and reports on educational institutions of Negroes and connected problems.

One of its first projects was an investigation of Negro institutions under the direction of the United States Office of Education. Dr. Thomas Jesse Jones' report, called "Negro Education," was published in two volumes, Bureau of Education Bulletin, Nos. 38 and 39, 1916. Another objective of the fund was to make appropriations to add to the salaries of Jeanes supervisors.

Most of the other activities of the Fund had little to do with education of the Negro in North Carolina, but did have far reaching

---

7. Dabney, Vol. II, pp. 451, 452.

8. Annual Reports, 1952-1955; Southern Educational Foundation, p. 11.

influence upon humanity generally.[9]

The Problem of Teacher Training

The foremost contributions of Newbold definitely was in the field of teacher training. The problem had been a serious one among white institutions as indicated in an earlier chapter. Certainly was this true in Negro schools; even down to the second and third decades of the present century teacher training had become the chief function of most of the higher institutions of Negro education.

When Mr. Newbold assumed the directorship of Rural Education of Negroes, he called a conference at Raleigh in December, 1913, to which seventy-five of the leading educators in North Carolina and Thomas Jesse Jones, of the Phelps-Stokes Fund, came. The object of the conference was the discussion of a course of study in the training of Negro rural teachers and to secure the cooperation of the four state institutions and the sixty-eight other schools and colleges in an incorporation of part or all of said course in their curriculum.[10]

The County Training School

The so-called "County Training School" had its inception in the intense desire of a county superintendent who wanted to raise the standard of teacher training by having one well graded school to which the best children would go from a one-teacher school and in which there might be some instruction of teachers for the small schools of the county.

In a certain county, of the 27 public school teachers only 2 had studied above the fifth grade. This was in 1911, the year which marks the beginning of the County Training School System. The Slater Fund would appropriate the sum of $500 if the counties would match this amount with the sum of $750 and aim to run the school for a term of ten months.[11]

Letters were sent by Dr. James Hardy Dillard, Agent of the Slater Fund, to state superintendents all over the South explaining the plan, to which the superintendents were receptive.

State Superintendent J. Y. Joyner of North Carolina wrote:

> I would approve most heartily your suggestion of a county industrial training school for Negro teachers. . . . I will take the matter up with Mr. N. C Newbold as soon as he takes charge of the work of supervising Negro rural schools in this state and cooperate with him in endeavoring to interest county superintendents and Boards of Education in this proposition.

9. Dabney, Vol. II, *Op. cit.*, pp. 456, 457.

10. Newbold, *Op. cit., Correspondence 1914.*

11. *Ibid.*

Of the county training schools, Mr. Newbold said in 1926 the following:

The establishing of the county training schools seemed a clear lead for the promotion of public high schools for Negro children. If the colleges were to prosper there must be a supply of secondary schools and a proper supply could come only through means of public funds.[12]

The objective of the County Training School was to develop high schools and teacher training. Yet at their inception none of them were high schools and superintendents did not want them called by false names as had been the case of some higher institutions which did little more than beginning high school work. So the name, "County Training School," was adopted.

Although aided by several sources or funds, the main development of the County Training School has been from public school funds. The number of county training schools grew from 4 in 1912 to 33 in 1928 and in that year the Slater Fund contributed to North Carolina county training schools $15,000. The Slater Board made the following proposition to Boards of Education relative to the county training school program:

The Slater Board would appropriate $500 a year for a teacher's salary on conditions

1. The property belong to the county, state, or district
2. That an appropriation for salary of not less than $1000 be made from public funds
3. That the term be at least 8 months
4. That teaching extend through the 8th grade with intentions to add 2 years as soon as possible

By 1926, there were in the South, 306 county training schools and 82 had reached a full four-year course.[13]

Effects

Just how effective the county training school program has been is difficult to appraise, but the following figures might help in the appraisal. In 1914-15 there were 1,934 one-teacher schools or 80%. In 1924-25 the number had been reduced to 1,263 or 52%; and in 1938-39 there remained only 656 one-teacher schools (30.6%) in the state. As to growth in teacher training, in 1924-25 there were 3,891 Negro teachers with only four years of high school training (or less) while in 1938-39 this category had been reduced to 255. In 1924-25 there were only 175 Negro teachers with four years' college training. By 1938-39 this category had increased to 7,113 teachers.[14]

---

12. *Ibid.*

13. *Ibid.*

14. Newbold, *Correspondence 1941*, Division of Negro Education.

In transportation, by 1928 thirty-one of the 129 rural schools of more than three teachers had bus transportation. The length of term of rural schools at the same time had reached 125.1 days.[15] (See later figures, Division of Negro Education February 14, 1958 in a later chapter.)

Supplementary Teacher Training

None of the activities of Newbold illustrate the far-sightedness of the man as did his far flung plan of raising the status of teachers already in service as well as for the prospective ones still in colleges and secondary institutions over the state.

So badly was the State in need of teachers during the early twenties, and, of course, prior to that time, superintendents could issue second grade certificates on the basis of examination in their offices. The result was that a great number of rural teachers fell into this category. Many of them had not had even a good grammar school education. Yet it must be said that many of them were consecrated to their tasks and succeeded in inspiring many of their proteges with noble aspirations.

The terms were so short, usually not more than six months, and salaries so low that few of these teachers could afford to attend regular summer schools.

Newbold carried the summer school to them. With aid from the General Education Board, so-called county summer schools were established in many counties and even at the State Normals a "county summer school" department was set up. Newbold secured the better trained and more experienced teachers for instructors at these county summer schools.

Teachers could advance from one sub-standard certificate to a higher certificate (Provisional C, B, and A) until a certificate equal to that granted a normal school graduate was obtained. A time limit was given teachers to reach the State Department's minimum certificate, Elementary "B," and those who could not or would not meet this requirement were gradually weeded out of the schools.

In the meantime the normal schools conducted "approved summer schools," which a graduate of a standard high school could attend and secure an Elementary "B" certificate. Continuing summer school at an "approved summer school" would enable the holder of a "B" certificate to obtain an "A" certificate.

In the course of the "twenties" the county summer school automatically ended, as all teachers had either gone beyond the status of provisional certificates or had retired from teaching.

The second method of Mr. Newbold's far flung program of teacher training was the establishing of teacher training departments in the private or church institutions. The support for this program came through regular funds of the State Board of Education.

---

15. Clement, Rufus E., *A History of Negro Education in North Carolina,* Unpublished Thesis, Northwestern University, 1930, p. 193.

Newbold secured able and experienced instructors, some of whom held graduate degrees in education and placed them in charge of the training of teachers. Some of these colleges had never set up professional teacher training and readily cooperated with the State Department through Mr. Newbold.

In 1921-22 eight institutions cooperated in training a total of 210 students in teacher training. In 1926-27 the following institutions cooperated in training a total of 334 students: Albion Academy, Bennett College, Biddle (Johnson C. Smith) University, Bricks Junior College, High Point, Livingstone, Kittrell, Durham, Shaw, and Mary Potter. An annual sum of $15,000 was appropriated in 1912 toward salaries of teachers who served as training instructors in private schools. In 1924-25 there were 3,891 Negro teachers with only high school training or less. By 1938-39 there were as few as 255 with only high school training. In the same period the number of Negro teachers with four years of college training increased from 175 to 3,974.[16]

Rosenwald School Program

Justice to the great benefactor of the Rosenwald schools impels us to give a brief statement of the life of Julius Rosenwald. Born in the land of Lincoln, at Springfield, Illinois, he early developed a zeal for the extension of the rights of citizenship to all men regardless of race. He grew up in affluence and in liberality toward the ignorant and the oppressed. Although a Jew, his philanthropies were without bias against any other religious sect. He gave to Catholic and to Protestant alike and to institutions abroad as well as at home.

He was a man with limited education but was foremost in civic pride and in righteousness for his city, threatened with evils which might have deterred lesser men. Rosenwald was honest, upright, and industrious having grown wealthy by his own energy and ingenuity. He died January 6, 1932, loved and honored by millions of every race which had benefited by his generosities.[17]

The Rosenwald School Fund was conceived in the mind of Julius Rosenwald by suggestions emanating from his association with Booker T. Washington at Tuskegee in 1912. Rosenwald was a trustee of Tuskegee Institute and upon visits at the famous institution saw, at first hand observation, the situation which served as a pattern for rural Negro schools in the South.

After a conference with President William Howard Taft, Andrew Carnegie, Booker T. Washington, and others a plan for building better school buildings for Negroes was adopted.[18]

---

16. Newbold Correspondence, *Op. cit.*

17. Dabney, Vol. II, pp. 473, 474.

18. *Ibid.*, p. 465.

Specifically a Rosenwald school was a Negro school building constructed with the aid of the Rosenwald Fund and according to specifications laid down by the Rosenwald Fund.

In the words of W. F. Credle, for years the North Carolina agent for the fund,

It seeks to embody the most modern principles of school hygiene and sanitation. It is required of the Directors of the fund that 2 acres on a public highway be secured: well drained with a supply of pure drinking water—2 sanitary closets approved by the Board of Health and steps to beautify the grounds.[19]

At the time of the above quotation by Mr. Credle (June, 1923) there were 300 Rosenwald schools in North Carolina located on sites ranging from 2 to 10 acres. They took the places of dilapidated schools often located on the edge of thickets or other undesirable places unsuited for play ground or agricultural work. A significant effect of the building of Rosenwald schools, said Credle, was to influence the erection of better buildings for white as well as Negro. Another important fact is that they encouraged better teachers who had been unwilling to go into rural districts and teach in buildings entirely inadequate in size, in state of repair, and in heating facilities.

Another effect of the Rosenwald school program was the building of teachers' homes which further attracted well trained teachers. In addition to providing suitable homes for teachers, these buildings served as models for better community homes. Still another effect was the improvement of morale among the Negroes. Patrons had contributed from their own personal funds; causing an interest in schools which would have been impossible without the stimulus furnished by Julius Rosenwald.[20]

Up to 1930 there had been 813 Rosenwald schools built in North Carolina. The enrollment in these schools totaled 114,210. The total cost amounted to $5,167,042.

Mr. Rosenwald died January 6, 1932. One year later the Fund brought to a conclusion its long program of aid in building school houses for Negroes in the southern states. It had aided in building 5,357 individual school houses in 883 counties in 15 southern states.

Let it be recognized that the Rosenwald Fund gave simply a part of the cost of these buildings as a stimulus to public authorities; to the Negroes themselves; and to local white friends. The main part of the funds came from public treasuries, although substantial amounts came from Negroes themselves; a striking evidence of the desire of the race for the schooling of its children.

---

19. Newbold Correspondence: *Report of W. P. Credle, Rosenwald Agent, 1923.*

20. *Ibid.*

Once erected, the buildings became a part of the public school system and were supported and maintained by public school authorities.[21]

Newbold and Negro Division of Education

A departure in southern state department circles was the establishment of the Negro Division of Education by Act of the General Assembly in 1921.[22]

Newbold, made the Director, set about immediately to strengthen high school training in urban centers as well as to continue his work of raising the standard of rural schools. He secured for his assistant an able educator in G. H. Ferguson, who succeeded to the directorship upon the retirement of Newbold in 1951. In addition to his assistant director, Newbold obtained an energetic and well trained supervisor of high schools in W. A. Robinson and an equally qualified and successful Jeanes supervisor, Mrs. Annie W. Holland, to supervise elementary schools of the state.

Before the 20's there were no high schools, as we know them, among Negroes in the state. True enough many of the larger towns and cities had incorporated many high school subjects in their curricula and actually gave diplomas for high school graduation. Some of them, like the colleges, were highly classical, but the idea of standardization in buildings, equipment, and proper certification of teachers was completely unknown.

In the colleges, secondary training was often blended with courses below and above high school and called, "academic." A student would usually have to spend one or more years in a college institution to complete his high school course.

The following tables give some indication of the number of high school students in some of the leading institutions for higher learning before standard high schools for Negroes existed. The figures represent the number of students enrolled for teacher training.[23]

21. Newbold Correspondence, 1938.

22. Clement, *Op. cit.*, p. 210.

23. Newbold Correspondence, 1921-45.

High School Enrollment and in Colleges 1921-22

Table I

| | HIGH SCHOOL | | | COLLEGE COURSE | | | | |
| | Year | | | Year | | | | |
Year	3rd	4th	Total	1st	2nd	3rd	4th	Total
National Training School (Durham)	0	15	15	0	0	0	3	3
Albion Academy	16	6	22					
Bennett College	14	25	39					
Biddle University	0	0	0	0	4	0	14	18
Livingstone	24	20	44	0	0	0	0	0
Bricks Junior College	11	10	21					
Shaw University	1	6	7	6	0	2	0	8
High Point Normal	2	7	9					
Kittrell College	15	21	36	0	0	2	42	44
TOTAL	83	110	193	6	4	4	59	73

Table II (1925-26)

	3rd	4th	Total	1st	2nd	3rd	4th	Total
Albion Academy	0	12	12					
Allen Home	0			3	6			6
Bennett College	0	14	14					
Biddle University (Johnson C. Smith)	Academy discontinued							
Bricks Junior College	18	4	22		0	24	17	41
Henderson Institute	0	8	8					
Hertford County Training School	0	0	0	14				14
High Point Normal	0	0	0					
Kittrell College	0	46	46					
Livingstone College	0	5	5	2	43	11	1	57
Mary Potter	Had become Durham Normal							
National Training School	10	0	10					
Peabody Academy	0	9	9					
Scotia Seminary	0	39	39					
Shaw University	Academy discontinued				10	35	42	87
TOTAL	28	137	165	28	53	70	60	211

From these figures it will be noted that in 1925-26 Shaw University and Biddle (Johnson C. Smith) University showed no high school students, having discontinued their academic departments. By this time high schools of standard grade had begun to sprout in many parts of the state.

Standard High Schools (1920 to 1940)

A standard high school is defined as a high school that presents the following minimum requirements: A school term of not less than 160 days, four years of grades of work beyond the seventh elementary grade, three teachers holding required certificates, not less than forty-five pupils in average daily attendance, a program of studies approved by the State Superintendent of Public Instruction, and such equipment as may be deemed necessary by the Superintendent of Public Instruction to make the instruction beneficial to pupils.[24]

These general criteria included adequate plants, science laboratories with minimum science facilities and equipment, libraries of 300 or more approved books, and a program of studes consistent with normal secondary school practice.

Before 1921 and the establishing of the Negro Division of Education, no Negro schools could comply with this standard. True, there were some high school courses offered in some of the larger schools, but practically all the secondary education Negroes received was in the colleges and in the numerous private or church schools.

Newbold and Standardization

Newbold, with the prophetic insight of an educational statesman, had already set in motion the normal corollary of standard facilities and equipment; that is, "standard" teachers. This had already been initiated with the county training school system. Through the aid of the General Education Board, he secured scholarships for worthy prospects to study for greater service as high schools were being standardized.

A second movement was to establish teacher training departments in the private institutions with financial assistance from the State Department. His able assistant, G. H. Ferguson, supervised the work in these institutions as well as in that of the summer schools. The result was almost a revolution in the improvement of teachers.

During the same period, Newbold secured an outstanding high school supervisor, W. A. Robinson, to work with the rapidly growing high schools. Robinson had worked in the high schools of Louisville, Kentucky, and was a highly trained expert in high school

---

24. Educational Publication Number 79; *Division of Supervision No. 30*, p. 7.

functions. His knowledge, experience, and diplomacy went far toward helping superintendents to standardize their Negro high schools.

A third factor which illustrates the far reaching statesmanship of Newbold was his inducement of the private secondary schools to turn their plants over to the state. No doubt Newbold was materially aided by the Jones Report of 1916[25] which showed so many inadequacies of the private schools.

Obviously few, if any of the private secondary schools, could meet the state requirements for standard high schools. However, to their undying credit, much good work was being done, but the securing of adequate standard equipment for most of them was quite prohibitive.

Conscientiously, year by year, Newbold counselled with church men, heads of these schools, and with the State Department of Public Instruction looking toward the assumption of these institutions by the state. By far, the majority of them were conducted by the Baptists. At the request of the State Department a poll was taken at the Baptist State Convention at Winston-Salem in 1925 as to whether these secondary schools could meet the standard requirement of the state. The vote was a decisive negative one. As a result all of the Baptist schools except Roanoke Institute, Elizabeth City, disposed of their properties or became parts of the public school system.[26]

One by one all other denominational secondary schools became the property of the state, thus completing a great triumph for Newbold and further accelerating the rapid advance of standardization of Negro high schools. In 1924-25 there were 21 public high schools and 22 private. In 1938-39 there were 153 public and only 5 private high schools. [27]

The rapid growth is reflected further in the following table:[28]

25. Dabney, Vol. II, *Op. cit.,* p. 450.

26. Graves, C. S. *The Negro Baptists of North Carolina,* p. 33.

27. Newbold Correspondence, *Op. cit.*

28. Division of Negro Education, *Some Facts About Negro Education,* February 14, 1958.

TABLE III
Number of High School Units by Size

Year	No. of 1-2 Tchr. Schs.	No. of 3-5 Tchr. Schs.	No. of 6-11 Tchr. Schs.	No. of 12-16 Tchr. Schs.	Above 16 Tchr. Schs.	Total No. Negro High Schs.
1921-30	44	52	23	13		119
1939-40	46	105	60	16		224
1949-50	24	97	85	26	13	235
1952-53	15	68	106	*12 or more* 48	21	236
1953-54	17	57	115	57		237
1954-55	13	45	120	62		235
1955-56	11	44	120	67		237
1956-57	14	32	128			241

Accreditation

High schools which complied with State Department requirements began to be accredited by the State Department as early as 1926 although the secondary department of Immanuel Lutheran College in Greensboro and Palmer Memorial Institute in Sedalia, both private institutions, were accrdedited in 1923 and Allen High in Asheville, also private, in 1924.

In 1957 there were 198 public high schools and 6 private high schools accredited by the State Department of Public Instruction. Of these 198 public high schools, 40 had been approved by the Southern Association of Colleges and Secondary Schools.[29]

The Southern Association is a rating agency which bases its approval upon the application of "Evaluative Criteria" developed from the cooperative Study of Secondary School Standards in 1935.[30]

The Study from which the criteria were evolved covers completely every phase of secondary education including the school's philosophy and objectives, its educational program, staff, plant, administration, and individual staff members.

To obtain approval of the Southern Association, an institution must first conduct an evaluation of itself with the use of the Evaluative Criteria. It then invites a committee of experts under State Department supervision which checks the institution's self evaluation.

High School Viewpoint

Before the era of the modern high school, secondary training was focused almost exclusively upon college entrance. Today, with less than 40% of high school graduates entering college, it is obvious that the objective had to be changed in order to serve the more than 60% who do not go to college.

Vocational agriculture for rural schools and diversified occupations, including vocational training for the city schools is now included in the curriculum of most of the larger high schools. For girls, courses in home making and in diversified occupations are being offered. To provide for college entrance, most high schools maintain parallel curricula in languages and social studies for one; science and mathematics for another; and commercial or business for a third curriculum.

In the best high schools the pupil activity program, consisting of various school functions such as athletics, band, glee club and other organizations, is included as curricular rather than extracurricular activities.

---

29. *Ibid.*

30. Cooperative Study of Secondary School Standards, *Evaluative Criteria,* 1940 Edition.

Dr. James B. Conant, president emeritus of Harvard University, has completed a two-year study of high schools in 26 states and summarized his findings in a book, "The American High School Today." He cautions against concentrating on the college-bound student at the expense of the boy or girl whose education will end with high school graduation. The minimum size of a high school graduating class should be 100 students. Allowing for drop-outs, this means a total enrollment of about 600 students and 24 teachers. This would permit a full curriculum, including both academic and vocational courses. The answer seems to be consolidation.

Commenting upon Conant's ideal, Dr. Charles F. Carroll, State Superintendent of Public Instruction, points out that North Carolina has made much progress in consolidation, for in 1930 there were 145 high schools in North Carolina with one or two teachers. In 1958 there were only 22 such high schools; while the number of 12 or more teachers (approaching Dr. Conant's ideal faculty size) increased in the same period from none to 294.[31]

Summary

The Era of Newbold has included greater strides and perhaps more profound development in the education of Negroes in North Carolina than has any other period of this study. It marked the establishment of the Jeanes Fund and the far-reaching activities of the Jeanes teachers; the expansion of the Slater Fund into the area of the county training school movement; the development of teacher training, the Rosenwald School Fund; the organizing of the Division of Negro Education; and the rapid development of standard high schools. In a later chapter some facts as to the development of elementary schools will be given, and the succeeding chapter will endeavor to tell the story of the establishment and growth of the colleges.

31. Munger, Guy, *Public Schools Making Gains*, Greensboro Daily News, February 22, 1959.

Chapter VI

The Colleges

From the early beginnings of education among Negroes in North Carolina, much of the teaching was spread over a great many subjects, some of which are still regarded as beyond the reach of Negro students or at least are thought to be useless to them. For instance, Latin, Greek and Hebrew were among the subjects taught especially to those aspiring to the ministry. Although some of them, perhaps, were seriously challenged by these subjects, we have known many of them who were profoundly scholarly and had quite mastered these more or less archaic subjects.

Of course, for the majority of these early Negro students, the teaching of the fundamental subjects of grammar and mathematics continued to be the main objective even of our leading institutions for many years, or until high schools began to develop as a basis for qualified college entrance.

The story in the chapter which follows attempts to portray the history behind the establishing of our colleges in North Carolina; noting particularly the pioneers who stood at their birth, and their successors who have brought them to the high standard they so nobly bear today.

Many of these pioneers were white; some of them were Negro. All of them made great sacrifices in establishing these institutions. Whites were ostracized; sometimes threatened, but persisted in their determination. Negro pioneers were without funds and often suffered serious personal deprivations, but they too endured to the end.

Negro students today should learn of these great and dedicated souls and should ever revere them for the role they played that Negroes should have a new birth of freedom and that their posterity might enjoy the blessings of a liberal education. This, then, is the aim of the chapter which follows.

Shaw University.

The birth of Shaw University had its inception in the activities of the Northern missionaries whose work has already been mentioned in the chapter on Education in the Transition Period between the Issuance of the Emancipation Proclamation and the Close of the Civil War.

A young chaplain, Henry Martin Tupper, was discharged from the Union Army on July 14, 1865, and, soon after, was asked by the American Baptist Home Mission Society to take up work as a missionary to the colored people.

Tupper selected Raleigh as a convenient center to begin his work. He preached in cabins and abandoned buildings and on December 1, 1865, organized a class in theology in the old Guion Hotel, situated where the State Museum now stands.[1]

With $500 he had saved while in the army, Tupper purchased a lot on the corner of Blount and Cabarrus Streets and there erected a two-story wood structure and named his institution, The Raleigh Institute. The original enrollment was 75, and the school's objective was the training of ministers and teachers.[2]

The present site of Shaw University was purchased in 1870. Through the generosity of Elijah Shaw, who contributed $8,000, Shaw Hall was erected, and the school assumed the name Shaw Collegiate Institute in honor of its largest donor.

Tupper established a brick yard from which students made the brick for this building.

Girls were admitted in 1870 when Estey Hall was made possible by a northern benefactor, Deacon Jacob Estey of Brattleboro, Vermont, who contributed most of the cost of the building.

In 1880, Judson Wade Leonard of Hamden, Massachusetts, gave $5,000 to establish a medical department and in 1881 the North Carolina Legislature gave the land for the erection of Leonard Hall. The first class entered the Medical school in 1881 and five years later, 1886, six were graduated. The medical faculty was composed entirely of southern white instructors.[3]

The institute was incorporated in 1875 as Shaw University. Aside from the courses in theology the early curriculum was adapted to the needs of the time which largely meant the training of teachers. The school of Pharmacy graduated its first class in 1893.

Charles F. Meserve, of Plymouth, Massachusetts, came as head of the institution in 1894. He set about to improve the physical plant by providing facilities for cooking, serving, dress making, laundry work and other domestic arts. An industrial building for boys was added.

---

1. Hartshorne, *Era of Progress and Promise*, p. 87. Shaw University Bulletin, p. 20.

2. Informationnaire—William R. Strassner, President 1958.

3. Hartshorne, *Op. Cit.*, p. 91.

The major work of Shaw during its early years was the training of teachers, although it maintained its collegiate, medical and theological courses. Most of the schools in the eastern part of the state looked to Shaw for their teachers, and at one time five of the seven normal schools were presided over by Shaw graduates.

Equally outstanding were graduates of its medical school. A. W. Benson, of the class of 1895, was the first Negro to obtain a license from the Virginia Medical Examiners. C. R. Alexander, also a Shaw graduate, was the first person of any race to receive 100 per cent in an examination before the Virginia Medical Board. He became chief surgeon of the Sixth Regiment of the United States Infantry during the Spanish-American War.[4]

About 1912 the medical course was reduced from four to two years, and in 1918 all professional departments were discontinued upon the recommendation of the President of the University.[5]

The University is supported by endowment and trust funds made possible chiefly by contributions of the General Education Board and the American Baptist Home Mission Society. It also receives support from the General Baptist State Convention of North Carolina, the American Baptist Board of Education, alumni, and more recently, the United Negro College Fund. The Southern Baptist Home Mission Board makes an annual contribution to the work of the Department of Religious Promotion.

Objectives.

That Religion and Learning may go hand in hand and character grow with knowledge.

The early objectives of the University were typical of the times: training of teachers, ministers, and nurses. Among the present: an environment in which students may be aided in their further intellectual, cultural and character development and consequent preparation for the most adequate possible adjustment to their future social environment; to provide preparation for elementary and high school teaching and for the Christian ministry; to provide pre-professional training for those who plan to pursue the study of medicine, dentistry, law, and other professions.

The philosophy underlying these objectives is that religion must be included as well as definite attention to all areas of individual aspirations for wholesome and serviceable lives.[6]

Expansion of Facilities.

Aside from the fourteen brick and four frame buildings on the main campus, the University in 1949 acquired the old Rex Hospital

---

4. J. A. Whitted, *Negro Baptist in North Carolina*, p. 153.

5. Caulbert A. Jones—The Shaw Bulletin, Vol. X, 1940, p. 14.

6. The Shaw Bulletin, Vol. XXVII, No. 1, 1957.

property from Wake County. This property comprises three building units and a heating plant Here are housed the administrative offices, Student Center, Art Gallery, Art Department, a small assembly room and a conference room.

The University also acquired from the State of North Carolina in 1949 five acres of property in Chavis Heights for the erection of a stadium.[7]

Presidents.

Throughout the history of Shaw University, six presidents have served the institution.

Henry Martin Tupper, the founder, served from 1865 to 1893; Charles Frances Meserve from 1894 to 1919; Joseph Leishman Peacock, 1920-1931; William Stuart Nelson became the first Negro President and served from 1931 to 1936; Robert Prentis Daniel from 1936 to 1950 and William Russell Strassner became President in 1951.[8]

Outstanding Graduates.

Among the many illustrious products of Shaw University are the following educators, now deceased: E. E. Smith, of Fayetteville State Normal (State Teachers College); P. W. Moore, Elizabeth City State Normal (State Teachers College); John Crosby, First President A. M. College (now A. & T.) Greensboro and James E. Shepard, founder of North Carolina College, Durham.

In addition and living at the time of this writing are: The Honorable Armond W. Scott, Judge, Municipal Court in Washington, D. C., Miss Angie Brooks, Assistant Attorney General, Monrovia, Liberia, and Dr. Wendell C. Somerville, Executive secretary of the Lott Carey Foreign Mission Convention of America.[9]

Saint Augustine's College.

That two well established and permanent institutions should have been set up in Raleigh seems only natural since Raleigh is the seat of the state government and so large a concentration of Negroes existed in that area at the close of the Civil War.

We have already noted the work of missionaries of several religious denominations in cooperation with the Freedmen's Bureau —The Baptists at Shaw University in Raleigh and the Presbyterians at Biddle University in Charlotte. Methodists are identified with Livingstone College in Salisbury and Bennett College in Greensboro.

---

7. *Ibid.* p. 25.

8. *Ibid.* p. 20.

9. Informationnaire, *Op. cit.*

The Episcopalians in cooperation with the Freedmen's Commission of the Protestant Episcopal Church and a group of clergy and laymen of the Diocese of North Carolina are credited with the founding of Saint Augustine's College. The chief influence was that of Bishop Thomas Atkinson, the first president of the Board of Trustees, and Rev. J. Brinton Smith, the first administrative head.[10]

The institution was established July 19, 1867, as Saint Augustine's Normal and Collegiate Institute. Its original objectives were: the training of teachers and the training of ministers; trades were later added, but were discontinued. In 1896 nurse training was added in connection with the adjacent Saint Agnes Hospital.

The objectives today have been simplified to teacher training, pre-theological, pre-medical and other pre-professional training.[11]

The institution was awarded the "A" rating by the North Carolina Department of Public Instruction in 1930 and at its 64th Commencement in 1931 conferred its first bachelor degrees. The college was accredited in 1933 by the Southern Association of Colleges and Secondary Schools and in 1942 was given Class "A" status by the American Medical Association. It is also a member of the Association of American Colleges, The American Council on Education, and the United Negro College Fund.

The institution's philosophy is based upon Christian values and Christian leadership beamed toward development of more useful and purposeful lives in our democratic society.

The first building was erected in 1868 and an extensive building program was carried on between 1881 and 1896. The enrollment started with four pupils in 1868 and reached an all time high of 500 in 1920.[12]

Outstanding graduates of Saint Augustine's College include: The Rt. Reverend Bradid W. Harris, Bishop of Liberia; Lloyd A. Quarterman, nuclear chemist and author; Dr. Howard McNeil, prominent surgeon and physician of Pontiac, Michigan, and member of the Board of Trustees; and Justice Hubert Delaney of the New York City Domestic Courts.[13]

The following have served as heads of the institution: The Rev. J. Brinton Smith, D.D., 1867-1872; the Rev. J. E. C. Smedes, D.D., 1872-1884; the Rev. Robert B. Sutton, D.D., 1884-1891; the Rev. A. B. Hunter, D.D., 1891-1916; the Rev. Edgar H. Goold, M. A., 1916-1947; Harold L. Trigg, Ed.D., 1947-1955; and James A. Boyer, Ed.D., 1955 to the present.[14]

---

10. Saint Augustine's Record 1957-58, p. 14.

11. Information—President James A. Boyer.

12. Saint Augustine's Record, *Op. cit.*, pp. 14-15.

13. Information—President James A. Boyer.

14. Saint Augustine's Bulletin, p. 15.

Johnson C. Smith University (Formerly Biddle University)

As Shaw University, in the East,, arose as an outcome of the Civil War, so in the West, arose Biddle University, a parallel to the birth of Shaw—one founded by the Baptists, the other by the Presbyterians; both dedicated to the training of ministers and teachers. Shaw was founded in 1865; Biddle in 1867.

Speaking at the Fiftieth Anniversary (1917) of the founding of Biddle, Dr. George E. Davis, of the class of 1883 remarked:

When I recall the days of small things—the early struggles, the trials, of my Alma Mater, known in my student days as Biddle Memorial Institute, and contrast that period with the present—Biddle Institute with Biddle University, with its commanding site, noble and attractive buildings, its able faculty and splendid equipment, its phenomenal developments and success, I instinctively exclaim: 'What hath God wrought.'[15]

The institution was formally started by the Catawba Presbytery in the old Charlotte Presbyterian Church, formerly located at the corner of D and Fourth Streets in Charlotte, April 7, 1867.[16] However, the institution had been chartered by the North Carolina Legislature in the spring of 1866.

The first teachers were the Reverends S. C. Alexander and W. L. Miller both ministers of the Southern Church and of the Concord Presbytery. The original name came in memory of the husband of Mrs. Henry J. Biddle who contributed $1,000 to the cause. Colonel Henry J. Biddle had fallen in battle in defense of the Union. Mrs. Biddle contributed an additional $400 on provision that the institution be chartered "The Henry J. Biddle Memorial Institute." She later contributed an additional $500 and continued to give until her death.[17]

The present site of the institution was the gift of Colonel W. R. Myers, a Southerner, patriot, and philanthropist; one whose intelligence and Christian principle were capable of rising above the prejudices of his times.[18]

The first building erected on the site given by Colonel Myers was the old Navy Building of the Confederacy, purchased for $150. Through the Freedmen's Bureau, the institution received $3,000 of unclaimed pension funds in 1867 and in 1869 received an additional $6,000. These funds were used in building homes for staff members.

15. Davis, George E., Address, *Fiftieth Anniversary of the Founding of Biddle University*, Johnson C. Smith University Bulletin, Vol. 8, No. 3, p. 39.

16. Smith Bulletin, Vol. 24, p. 17.

17. Smith Bulletin, Vol. 8, No. 3, p. 41.

18. *Ibid.*, p. 41.

In June 1869, the Reverend Stephen Matoon, D.D. of New York succeeded Rev. Mr. Alexander as President. Matoon had been a missionary in Siam.[19]

In 1877 the charter was changed by the Legislature of North Carolina and the name became Biddle University. It operated under this name until 1923, when because of the great benefactions of Mrs. Jane Berry Smith, of Pittsburgh, the name was changed to Johnson C. Smith University in memory of her late husband. From 1923 until her death Mrs. Smith gave funds for the erection of five additional buildings, altogether nine buildings including the Memorial Gate to the campus.

In 1932 the charter was amended to admit women and the university has since been coeducational. The present site contains seventy-five acres of land and twenty-two buildings.[20]

The university was the first major Negro institution to be administered by a Negro president. As early as 1891 the Reverend Daniel J. Sanders, D.D. was elected its first colored President.[21] After him are the following able and illustrious leaders: Dr. H. L. McCrorey, D.D., L.L.D., Dr. Hardy Liston, Dr. J. W. Seabrook (acting) and Dr. R. P. Perry, the present President (1959).

The early objectives—the training of teachers, ministers, Sunday School workers and church missionaries—are combined into those of the present: "All professions and Christian vocations." The enrollment at the beginning was 75. It had reached 854 in 1958. The approximate value of all facilities of the University totaled $3,000,-000 in 1958.

Some of the outstanding alumni of the University include the following: Armond W. Scott, class of 1896, retired Judge, Municipal Courts, Washington, D. C.; J. W. Seabrook, class of 1909, retired President of State Teachers College, Fayetteville, N. C.; Lewis K. Downing, class of 1916, Dean of the Howard University School of Engineering and Architecture, Washington, D. C.; L. S. Cozart, class of 1916, President of Barber-Scotia College, Concord, N. C.; James Vance McIver, class of 1919, Pastor of the Union Baptist Church, Orange, New Jersey and member of the General Assembly of New Jersey; Ernest C. Grigg, Jr., class of 1932, United States Social Welfare Adviser to the Middle East; Albert E. Manley, class of 1930, President of Spellman College, Atlanta, Ga.; Matthew J. Whitehead, class of 1930, Director of the Graduate School, District of Columbia Teachers College, Washington, D. C.; Charles W. Baulknight, class of 1935, Physical Chemist-Aerophysics Section of the Aerodynamics Laboratory Operation, Philadelphia, Pa., and President of the General Alumni Association of Johnson C. Smith

19. *Ibid.*, p. 44.

20. Smith Bulletin, Vol. 24, p. 18.

21. *Ibid.*, p. 44.

University; and R. P. Perry, class of 1925, President of Johnson C. Smith University, Charlotte, N. C.[22]

Bennett College For Women.

The only institution for higher learning strictly for women is Bennett College, located in Greensboro, North Carolina, founded in 1873 by the Methodist Episcopal Church. It was organized as a co-educational school and remained so until 1926 when it was reorganized as a college for women. Its first administrative head was Edward O. Thayer.

As with most of the institutions founded for the Negro during the early years of freedom, the objectives of Bennett College included the training of teachers and ministers. While its current objectives are in the field of high school and elementary teacher training, they are far reaching in the cultural and esthetic development of the finer qualities of womanhood.[23]

The Institution's own expression in its statement of purpose is a basis for the broad objectives which characterize Bennett College today.

Our purpose is to meet the developing needs of young women through a unique program of individual instruction undergirded by rich experiences in group participation and community living.

The objectives are simple and concise:

To provide opportunities for growth in religious thought to the end that Christian principles will be made to occupy a definite place in the experience of the student;

To provide the environment and facilities that will make for the physical fitness of the student and develop in her an appreciation for a healthy mind and body;

To promote straight thinking and enlightened understanding—characteristics of an informed and disciplined mind;

To insure adequate preparation in specialized fields that will make possible the successful pursuit of a given vocation;

To provide ample opportunities and experiences in daily living that will stimulate practice in the art and science of home living;

To develop an understanding of an appreciation for the cultural and scientific achievements of man;

To develop the desire to aid in the solution of social problems by critical and unemotional analysis of current social issues;

To stimulate an appreciation for the beautiful in every day living as well as in the arts;

22. Perry, Dr. R. P., *Presidential Informationnaire.*

23. Informationnaire, Mary L. Mayfield, Registrar, Bennett College 1959.

To provide varied types of recreation to satisfy the need for play and to give direction in the proper use of leisure time.[24]

Early History

Lyman Bennett, of Troy, New York, gave the first large sum, $10,000, toward the founding of the institution. Hence the name, Bennett College. It was chartered as a college by the North Carolina Legislature in 1889. Most of its courses at the time were of a classical emphasis and most of its students were preachers and teachers. The physical plant expanded rapidly from five buildings in 1881 to twenty-three in 1900. At this time the institution was committed to coeducational functions.

Although a chartered college, it admitted students to grades as low as the sixth, but the emphasis was upon secondary and normal training. Needless to say that the day of standardization had not arrived for colleges of the Negro race.

Among the administrative heads of Bennett College were Edward O. Thayer, already mentioned as the first; J. D. Chavis, 1900; Silas Peeler, 1911; J. E. Wallace, 1915; and Frank Trigg, 1917, who is said to have built Jones Hall, one of the finest dormitories at the time, and also the present Administration Building.[25] David D. Jones came on the scene in 1926 as the institution was being converted into a college for women. Upon the death of Jones in 1956, Willa B. Player became the first woman to head a college of the Negro race in North Carolina.[26]

The New Bennett College

In 1926 the Board of Education of the Methodist Episcopal Church and the Woman's Home Missionary Society of the M. E. Church decided to operate a college for women and selected Bennett as the most suitable for this innovation in the education of Negro women.[27]

Bennett College today is best remembered by the part played by David D. Jones, who succeeded Frank Trigg in 1926. Under his leadership the institution expanded rapidly both as to its physical facilities and its professional potentialities as a college for women. By 1930 the college had an "A" rating by the North Carolina State Department of Public Instruction and by 1935, a rating of "A" by the Southern Association of Colleges and Secondary Schools.

Generous contributions from the family of Henry Pfeiffer of New York and also from the General Education Board enabled the

24. Bennett College Bulletin, 1958-60, pp. 9, 10.

25. Information, H. L. Trigg, Teacher at Bennett 1913-1916.

26. Miscellaneous Bennett College Bulletins (compiled) 1900-1940.

27. Bennett College Bulletin 1940-1941.

WILLA B. PLAYER

*First Woman President of
Bennett College*

college to erect thirteen substantial buildings aside from a home for the President and other residences on the campus.[28]

David Jones died in 1926 with a miraculous record of transformation of a compact and beautiful college campus. A single sentence from a leading daily newspaper is a good epitome of the role of David D. Jones:

> Jones is thought of primarily as builder of Bennett College which will ever stand as his greatest memorial.[29]

Some of the outstanding products of Bennett College are: Bishop Robert E. Jones, of the Methodist Episcopal church; Madie Ruth Gamble-Norman, actress; Barbara E. Crutchfield, Attorney-at-law and Teacher of Law at the University of Hawaii; Myrtle Brown, Nutritionist, U. S. Department of Agriculture, Washington, D. C.; Vermelie Kelly Piper, M.D., Physician-Pediatrician; and Miriam McTeer, Head of Department of Home Economics at Tennessee A. and I. University, Nashville, Tennessee.[30]

Livingstone College

Of the existing colleges of the Negro race in North Carolina, the first to be started exclusively by Negroes was Livingstone, located at Salisbury. The beginnings of Livingstone College had its seed sown in the city of Fayetteville, but came up in Concord and grew to maturity in Salisbury. The establishing of the institution is inextricably linked with the name of Joseph Charles Price, perhaps the foremost orator of his day.

In the establishing of Livingstone, it is observed again that religious emphasis has been the real basis of the education of the Negro; for it was through the efforts of the Methodists (A.M.E. Zion), like the Baptists for Shaw, the Presbyterians for Biddle, and the Episcopalians for Saint Augustine's, that Livingstone was established.

Efforts had been made by the A.M.E. Zion church to set up a college at Fayetteville as early as 1876, but the State Normal School took the chosen leader and the movement was transferred to Concord, where an institution named Zion Wesley Institute was established in 1870.[31]

Although Price is generally credited with the founding, Bishop Walls says that C. R. Harris was its first principal.[32] The school was moved to Salisbury in 1882. Its original site of forty acres was on land known as "Delta Grove." Through the influence of Lee S.

28. *Ibid.*

29. Greensboro Daily News, January 26, 1956.

30. Informationnaire, *Op. cit.*

31. Informationnaire, Julia B. Duncan, Registrar, Livingstone, 1958.

32. Walls, William Jacob, *Joseph Price*, pp. 227-28.

JOSEPH CHARLES PRICE, *Founder*
Livingstone College

Overman (later to become U. S. Senator) a charter was secured in 1883 and the institution formally became Zion Wesley Institute.[33]

The change to Livingstone College came about in the following manner: Among the 13,000 Union soldiers buried in the graveyard of a former Confederate prison, was found the grave of a son of David Livingstone. The recollection of the missionary activities of the father and the sacrifice by his son for Negro freedom greatly impressed the church leaders, especially Bishop J.W. Hood, who induced the Legislature to issue a new charter and the institution became Livingstone College in 1887.[34]

The original objectives of the institution follows closely the pattern of the earlier institutions in the training of teachers and ministers. They are essentially the same today but have been extended to the far reaches of the Continent of Africa from where many students come annually to "bask in the benign educational atmosphere of Livingstone College."

Role of Price

In 1881 Price was sent as a delegate to the Ecumenical Conference which met in England. His eloquent oratory made a deep impression upon the people of the British Isles and he was able to raise $10,000 for the establishment of an institution of higher learning. Upon his return in 1882 he was elected President of the institution.[35]

Price realized the difficulty of getting philanthropic support for a classical college for Negroes and he tried to make Livingstone a bridge between two extreme views of education. He therefore established courses in industries and home activities for women.

In interpreting the situation at the General Conference at New Bern in 1888, Price said: "The necessity of a connectional school not only for normal and academic culture, but also for theological training and industrial development admits of no argument. . . . Livingstone College stands before the world today as the most remarkable evidence of self-help among Negroes in this country.[36]

Price was able to secure aid from great philanthropists such as Collis P. Huntington, who gave a thousand dollars towards the cost of a chapel and dining hall; and Leland Stanford, who gave a brick building, a girls' dormitory which bears his name.

A year before his untimely death in 1893, Price reported that Livingstone had sixty-one graduates from thirteen states; that there were four large brick buildings and two smaller frame buildings on a campus of fifty acres.

---

33. Catalogue of 1884-85, Livingstone College, pp. 23-27.

34. *Ibid.*, Walls, pp. 251, 226.

35. Diamond Jubilee Bulletin 1957, Years of Progress June 1957.

36. Walls, *Op. cit.*, p. 252.

Price died at the early age of thirty-nine, but in that brief span, had so thoroughly established the institution that its permanence was secure. It received no state or Federal aid, depending solely upon private philanthropy and the A.M.E. Zion church, which was its sponsor. The approximate value of the entire facilities in 1958 was $1,840,968.[37]

Role of Aggrey

James E. K. Aggrey, an African who came to Livingstone at the age of twenty-three on a Bishops' Scholarship, was graduated from the college in 1902. He remained at the college as a teacher and influential leader for more than twenty years, when he returned to his native land to continue his educational activities in Africa. He is credited with being "The Father of African Education." Among those inspired by Aggrey is the present Prime Minister of Ghana, Kwame Nkrumah.[38]

Many high churchmen of the A.M.E. Zion connection have been identified in one way or another with the annals of Livingstone College. Aside from the pioneer church-statesman, Bishop J. W. Hood, the following are noteworthy: Bishop J. W. Walls, who was graduated from the college in 1908 and for many years has been a presiding Bishop of the A.M.E. Zion church and Bishop Alexander Walters, who was the first President of the Pan African Conference and also a presiding bishop of the A.M.E. Zion church.[39]

The administrative heads of the institution enjoyed rather long tenure. Joseph C. Price, 1879-1893; William Goler, 1893-1917; David C. Suggs, 1917-1925; and William J. Trent, 1925-1958.

Trent retired in 1958 because of physical disabilities and advanced age. Samuel E. Duncan, who had been a high school principal and State Supervisor of High Schools was elected President in 1958. Duncan is a graduate of Livingstone in the class of 1927.

Graduates of Livingstone are found in responsible positions in schools and colleges of America and in Africa. Aside from the educational field, they are serving in many other capacities. A few of the outstanding ones are listed: Rufus E. Clement, Class of 1919, now President of Atlanta, University, Atlanta, Georgia; Ruth Whitehead-Whaley, 1919, Attorney-at-Law and Secretary of the Board of Estimates, New York City; W. J. Trent, Jr., Class of 1930, Executive Director, United Negro College Fund; Felix S. Anderson, Member of the Kentucky State Legislature; and Charles Acolatse, a Judge in Ghana, Africa.[40]

---

37. Informationnaire, *Op. cit.*

38. Article on Aggrey, Ebony Magazine, April, 1959.

39. Walls, *Op. cit.*, p. 114.

40. Diamond Jubilee Bulletin, *Op. cit.*

SAMUEL E. DUNCAN
President, Livingstone College
1958-

Nestled in Concord near the heart of the city is picturesque Barber-Scotia College: formerly Scotia Seminary, the first institution in the State founded exclusively for the training of Negro women.

The institution was established by Luke Dorland in 1867 and called Scotia after his native Scotland. Dorland was commissioned by the Presbyterian church, U. S. A.,[41] to establish an institution for women and for many years Barber-Scotia has been a popular school among ambitious young women of other states as well as among many in North Carolina. Mary McLeod Bethune, famed founder of Bethune-Cookman College in Florida, was proud of her "Scotia Heritage." Speaking before a convention of the North Carolina Teachers Association, Mrs. Bethune remarked, "When I entered Scotia Seminary, for the first time in my life I went upstairs."

Scotia was incorporated in 1870 for the purpose of training women leaders in the education of and social service for their race.

Two important changes have influenced the growth of this institution. In 1916 the name was changed to Scotia Women's College and in 1930 it was merged with Barber College of Anniston, Alabama, and assumed its present name Barber-Scotia College.[42]

In 1954 its charter was amended to permit consideration of applications without regard to race or sex. The institution is fundamentally a liberal arts college with offerings looking toward the teaching profession.[43]

Barber-Scotia is accredited by and is a member of the Southern Association of Colleges and Secondary Schools. It offers courses leading to the Bachelor of Science degrees and contains ten departments: Fine Arts, Business Education, English Language and Literature, Education, Foreign Language, Home Economics, Natural Science, Social Studies, Physical and Health Education, and Religious Education.[44]

Aside from the support it receives from the Presbyterian Church, U. S. A., the institution receives substantial support by virtue of membership in the United Negro College Fund. The approximate value of its entire facilities is one and one-fourth million dollars. Its enrollment in 1958 was 240.[45]

Of the many outstanding graduates of the college, Mary McLeod Bethune was perhaps the most widely known, but many able though less widely known have taken leading roles in many walks

41. Hartshorne, W. N., *Era of Progress and Promise*, 1863-1910, p. 204.

42. Barber-Scotia College Bulletin 1957-58, p. 9.

43. Informationnaire, Dr. L. S. Cozart, President Barber-Scotia College.

44. Greensboro Daily News—School and College Section, April 13, 1959, p. B-7.

45. Informationnaire, *Op. cit.*

of life. Among them are Bessie Alberta Johnson-Whitted,[46] long time assistant treasurer and cashier of the North Carolina Mutual Life Insurance Company of Durham; Dr. Sarah B. Cordery; Professor Evelyn Davidson White, Dr. Thelma Davidson Adair, Astea S. Campbell, Rosa Gray, Charity Hatcher, and Susie Faucette, the last three, co-workers in the school system with the author.[47]

The names of the administrators, following the founder, Luke Dorland, follow: D. J. Satterfield 1886-1909; A. W. Verner 1907-1923; T. R. Lewis 1923-29; M. J. Crocker, 1929-1932, and the present head, Leland Stanford Cozart, who became president in 1932.[48]

Cozart, well trained in the liberal arts and with a well grounded philosophy of education, taught at Mary Potter High School in Oxford under its founder, G. C. Shaw. He later became Principal of Washington High School in Raleigh, was elected the first Executive Secretary of the North Carolina Teachers Association and for years has served as secretary-treasurer of the Association of Colleges and Secondary Schools.

Kittrell College

The African Methodist Episcopal Church established Kittrell College in 1886 in the little town of the same name.

A Miss Louise Dorr, a faithful northern teacher, was conducting Bible classes in Raleigh when some of the students became enthusiastic over their studies and started talk for better facilities. The leading spirit in the movement was one R. H. W. Leak who introduced the problem to the African Methodist Episcopal Church. The 1885 conference of this church adopted resolutions authorizing the establishing of a normal and industrial school.

The nearby Virginia Conference of the A.M.E. connection transferred its interest to the Kittrell project because of the desirability of its location. By 1892 at Philadelphia, the General Conference of the A.M.E. Church added Maryland and the District of Columbia to the area supporting Kittrell Institute as it was then called.[49]

John R. Hawkins was made Principal. Others who subsequently served as head of the institution were J. S. Williams, P. W. Dawkins, J. T. Wheeler, C. G. O'Kelley and G. A. Edwards. The present head is M. A. Camper

During the Newbold Era of the 20's Kittrell College declined because of a lack of financial means to meet standardization, but for some years operated a school for ministers and more recently a school of junior college level.

Its nearness to the State of Virginia enabled some parents in

---

46. Editorial, Carolina Times, Durham, August 8, 1959.

47. Recollections—The Author.

48. Information—L. S. Cozart, President Barbor-Scotia College, August, 1959.

49. Hartshorne, W. N., *Era of Progress and Promise*, pp. 288-89.

areas of that State where schools had been closed to take advantage of Kittrell College's facilities by enrolling their children in that Institution. One other notable contribution of the institution was that of giving seven or more acres of land to Vance County for a public high school.[50]

Immanuel Lutheran College

Immanuel Lutheran College owes its origin to the demand for God-fearing Negro teachers and ministers. Established in Concord in 1903, the institution was moved to its present location, Greensboro, in 1905. The first administrative head was N. J. Bakka. The Sponsorship for the institution was the Lutheran Synodical conference of North America and it is operated today by the Evangelican Luthern Synodical conference which comprises the Lutheran church-Missouri Synod, the Evangelical Lutheran Synod of Wisconsin and other states, the Norwegian Synod of the American Evangelical Lutheran church and the Slovak Evangelical Lutheran church.

The plant contains thirteen acres of land, several substantial buildings, and a small enrollment of 93 in 1957-58. The institution is coeducational and open to any one irrespective of race or religious affiliations. The chief objective is to provide a liberal and practical training for young men in the ministry and gifted girls who desire to enter the service of the church as Christian school teachers.[51]

Following Niels J. Bakka, the first head of the college, were Frederick Berg, D.D., who was president from 1911 to 1919; John Phillip Smith 1919-25; Henry Nau 1925-49; and William Kampschmitt, the present head of the institution.[52]

Some of the graduates of the college are the Reverend Osborn Smallwood, Ph.D., Associate professor of English at Howard University; the Reverend Peter Hunt, Dean of Alabama Lutheran Academy and College at Selma, Alabama; and Roland De Lomba, Ph.D., Associate Professor of English at Texas Southern University.[53]

State Institutions

The institutions heretofore discussed were all established and supported by various religious denominations and, except for some teacher training functions, received no public funds. In the early years of the Newbold era, the teacher training program with full

---

50. Informationnaire—C. C. Paschall, Principal Kittrell Public School.

51. Hartshorne, W. N., *Era of Progress and Promise;* 1863-1910, p. 365. Informationnaire report, Rev. William H. Kampschmitt, President, 1958.

52. General catalogue, Immanuel Lutheran College, 1954-56, p. 5.

53. Informationnaire, *Op. cit.*

state support was carried on in certain of the private colleges and secondary schools during a ten-year period from 1921 to 1931; the following institutions participating: Biddle University, Livingstone College, Albion Academy, Kittrell College, Brick School, High Point Normal Institute, National Training School (Durham) and Shaw University. In 1926 the following institutions were added: Peabody Academy, Scotia Seminary, Henderson Normal and Allen Home of Asheville. Most of this state support was discontinued in the 30's and gradually the colleges set up their own Departments of Education financed through their regular budgets.[54]

This section will be devoted to the story and contribution of the public supported institutions of higher learning.

Normal Schools

Many of the early institutions had the term "Normal" in their names. This term seemed to indicate that they were teacher training schools. Many also employed the term "Normal-Industrial" which often qualified them for aid from philanthropic sources.

At one time there were at least seven normal schools in the state which were largely state maintained even though some had been privately established. Among those no longer in existence are Plymouth Normal, established by H. C. Crosby in 1881; Salisbury Normal, founded by John O. Crosby; Franklinton Normal 1894; and Goldsboro Normal 1880.[55] Three others which today are well established Teachers Colleges are Fayetteville, Winston-Salem, and Elizabeth City state teachers colleges.[56]

Fayetteville State Teachers College

As early as 1867 a school building was erected on Gillespie Street in Fayetteville and called the "Howard School" after General O. O. Howard, Head of the Freedmen's Bureau which contributed most of the funds for the school.[57]

From the files of the State Superintendent's Correspondence 1868-1879 is found a petition for aid of the Peabody Fund to help the Howard School. This petition was sent August 19, 1875, to Dr. Barnas Sears, agent of The Peabody Fund, by George C. Scurlock, J. W. Hood, and James N. Lee School Committee. The teachers listed on the petition are Robert Harris, Principal, Mary Harris, and Susan Perry.[58]

---

54. Information, G. H. Ferguson, Director Negro Division State Department of Public Instruction, Raleigh.

55. Catalog, 1887, Superintendents' Files Miscellanoues Negro schools. Biennial Report 1894-96, State Superintendent.

56. Superintendents' Files, Miscellaneous Negro Schools.

57. N. C. Newbold, *Five Negro Educators*, p. 123. State Teachers College catalog 1957-58, p. 18.

58. Superintendents' Correspondence 1868-79.

Robert Harris, who was being sought by the AME Zion Church to head the future Livingstone College, became the first head of Fayetteville State Normal in 1876. He was followed by Charles W. Chestnut, a distinguished writer.

Although this institution was guided by two distinguished educators, its story is inextricably wrapped about the life of Ezekiel Ezra Smith who became its principal in 1883 and, except for two leaves of absence as a diplomat to Liberia and as an adjutant of the Third North Carolina Infantry, served as principal-president until his death in 1932.

During Smith's absence as Minister to Liberia, George H. William served as principal and while he was serving as Adjutant with the Third N. C. Volunteer regiment, R. E. Fairley served as principal.[59]

Smith presided over the institution for fifty years and saw its greatest expansion in the twilight of his career when upwards to ten well planned buildings were erected and the institution gradually developed into a teachers college.

The institution continued its expansion under J. Ward Seabrook, who succeeded Smith in 1933; and in 1939 by Legislative Act, it became Fayetteville State Teachers College with a full four-year college curriculum.[60]

Seabrook, an able administrator, saw nine buildings erected during his presidency. He retired in 1956 only to be called to the presidency of Johnson C. Smith University upon the passing of Hardy Liston, president of that institution. After serving one year as interim president, Seabrook retired to his home in Fayetteville.

Rudolph Jones, who rose from the high school teacher-principal ranks, became the president of the institution upon the retirement of Seabrook in 1956. He assumed the presidency of a plant valued at three million dollars and an enrollment of more than five hundred students. Two additional objectives had been added under Jones' administration; secretarial science and auto-mechanics.[61]

The institution in 1958 was valued at $3,000,000 and had an enrollment of five hundred students. Its graduates have filled teaching positions with distinction in many schools of the state. Some of the most outstanding are listed below:

J. S. Perry, Washington, D. C., successful physician, psychiatrist, author of professional articles in psychiatry. In addition, he has published a volume of poems and is an accomplished violinist.

59. Information—J. W. Seabrook, Former President State Teachers College, Fayetteville.

60. State Teachers College catalog, Op. cit., p. 18.

61. Informationnaire, Rudolph Jones, President State Teachers College, Fayetteville.

EZEKIAL EZRA SMITH
Fayetteville

Malcolm D. Williams, Ph.D., now Professor of Education at Tennessee State University, formerly professor at Shaw and Saint Augustine's College, and prior to that principal of a public school in Wilson. While at Teachers College, Columbia University, New York, he was elected president of the Student Council, being the first Negro to hold this job.

Fannie L. Taylor Johnson, Principal of a public school in Washington, D. C., formerly a teacher in Rocky Mount, N. C.

Lafayette Parker, Dean of State Teachers College, Fayetteville. Rose from the rank of a private to captain in World War II. Received doctor's degree from University of Pittsburgh. Holds offices in the N. C. Teachers Association (Head of Higher Education Department).

J. W. Smith (deceased), Bishop of the A. M. E. Zion Church.[62]

Elizabeth City State Teachers College

As Fayetteville was the embodiment of the life of E. E. Smith, so was Elizabeth City the personification of P. W. Moore. An exception is the fact that whereas Smith inherited the institution at Fayetteville, Moore actually established the institution at Elizabeth City.

The General Assembly of 1891 appropriated a sum of nine hundred dollars for the establishment of a normal school at Elizabeth City. This was supplemented by a sum of from one to two hundred dollars by the Peabody Fund.[63]

Moore was recommended by H. C. Crosby, principal of the Plymouth State Normal. F. F. Cahoon of Elizabeth City, Chairman of the State Board of Education, consulted Major S. M. Finger, State Superintendent of Public Instruction, about the qualifications of Moore. Major Finger highly recommended him in these words:

> I have observed this young man carefully and I believe you can make no mistake in selecting him to lead this school.[64]

At the time of the selection of Moore to head the institution, there was not even a site located. Moore and his assistant, J. H. Butler, obtained a building on what was known as Body Road Street and there on January 4, 1892, he established the State Normal School,

---

62. Information—J. W. Seabrook, Retired President State Teachers College, Fayetteville.

63. Superintendent Correspondence—State Department Archives, Miscellaneous Negro Schools, 1867-1909.

64. N. C. Newbold, *Five North Carolina Negro Educators*, p. 94.

P. W. Moore, *Founder*
State Normal School
Elizabeth City State Teachers College

now Elizabeth City State Teachers College. The name was changed by Legislative Act in 1893 to Elizabeth City Colored Normal and Industrial Institute.[65]

The school soon outgrew its original facilities and in 1894 the trustees secured a larger building formerly occupied by a parochial school conducted by northern missionaries. The school remained there until 1912 when it was moved to its present site.[66]

School heads today can scarcely realize the difficulties which confronted educators like Moore and Smith in the early days of our State schools.

From an address of P. W. Moore, found in the files of State Superintendent, S. M. Finger, we get an insight into a type of difficulty which many early educators bore:

> The Principal would be grateful to the Superintendent and the Board for advice as to how he might avoid dispensing with a part of his salary to meet emergencies that arise in school yearly. Prominent among them are several cases of illness where a physician must be summoned; and in cases of smallpox, when it becomes necessary for nearly a hundred students to be vaccinated. After recovering from severe illness, physicians usually advise that I send those students home where they may have the attention of their parents.

Moore's salary in 1905 was $700 a year.

Continuing, he wrote:

> The most essential needs of the school are dormitories, especially one for girls. As it is, I secured homes for all, in such places as I should like for them to stay, with great difficulty and sometimes under conditions that are not very favorable.

Moore realized also the difficult problem of educating boys—

> There is no industrial or manual training for boys. So far, about all I can do for the boys along practical lines is to teach them to sweep the rooms, cut wood, make fires, nail on boards, and keep the yards clean. Some of the boys are very industrious and desire that they have the opportunity to learn some trades. I am trying to convince our students and people that education must be coupled to something in order to be useful and valuable.[67]

By 1921 the normal schools began a program looking toward standardization. The high school courses were gradually discontinued as these institutions became standard two-year normal schools. At Elizabeth City in 1921, John H. Bias, a former teacher

---

65. Elizabeth City State Teachers College Bulletin, p. 11.

66. North Carolina Newbold, *Op. cit.*, p. 98.

67. Superintendent Correspondence, *Op. cit.*

at Shaw University and former principal of a county-training school, came as the first dean of the institution. He relieved Dr. Moore of the many pressing details of the school.

Moore retired in 1928 and Bias became head of the institution.[68] New buildings were erected and the normal program became a four-year teachers college with the name being changed to Elizabeth City State Teachers College by act of the General Assembly on March 28, 1939.

Harold L. Trigg, served as president from 1939 to 1945; Sidney D. Williams from 1945 to 1958 when Walter N. Ridley became the fifth head of the institution.[69]

While the main objective has always been the training of teachers, the present program includes secretarial science, brick masonry, cosmetology, and electronics. The enrollment in 1958-59 was 475 and represented the states of Virginia, Maryland, New York, New Jersey, Georgia, South Carolina, North Carolina, and the District of Columbia.

Its graduates are found teaching in the schools of many communities and many are known to be outstanding in their fields. A few well-known are listed: Martin Luther Wilson, Principal of Richard B. Harrison High School, Selma, North Carolina, and member of the College's Board of Trustees; William Green, Dean of Men, Fisk University; and John C. Bias, Principal, Brawley High School, Scotland Neck and President of the College Alumni Association.[70]

Winston-Salem Teachers College

Like E. E. Smith at Fayetteville and P. W. Moore at Elizabeth City, S. G. Atkins was the spark that ignited the flame of learning at Winston-Salem. He was the sum of ambition and success; for in his early days he aspired to be a good teacher, while in his latter years he saw the institution he founded reap the harvest of his persistent efforts.

Resigning from Livingstone College where he had taught for six years, Atkins established a school called Slater Industrial Academy in 1892.[71] The name was in honor of John F. Slater, the philanthropist, who created the Slater Fund for industrial education of Negroes.

The Legislature of 1895 passed an act to establish a normal school at or near Winston-Salem in Forsyth County for the training of colored teachers. The act further provided:

That for the purpose of aiding the Slater Industrial School located near said town and for securing for the use

---

68. Newbold, *Op. cit.*, p. 105.

69. Elizabeth City State Teachers College Bulletin, p. 11.

70. Informationnaire—Walter N. Ridley, President.

71. Catalog, State Teachers College 1930-31, p. 15.

S. G. ATKINS, *Founder*
Slater Normal, now Teachers College
Winston-Salem

of the State, the buildings erected and now used by the Slater Industrial School, the State Treasurer shall pay to the State Board of Education out of any funds in the treasury not otherwise appropriated, a sum equal in amount to the sum annually raised by the trustees and officers of Slater Industrial School, provided the sum does not exceed in any one year a thousand dollars.

Under this act Slater Normal School was established and opened in 1895 with S. G. Atkins as Principal and with seventy-six pupils representing seven counties in North Carolina and some students from the State of Virginia.

The chief objectives of Slater were stated in the Biennial Report of the State Superintendent of Public Instruction for 1894-96 as follows:

A thorough grounding of the students pursuing a normal course in the subjects they will teach in the public school.

A thorough acquaintance with the underlying principles of the sciences and art of education as illustrated in the best schools, together with a careful investigation of the facts and peculiarities of child nature.[72]

For several years in the early 1900's Atkins was "borrowed" by the A.M.E. Zion Church and C. G. O'Kelley served as principal in the interim. Atkins was secretary of education for the A.M.E. Zion Church and represented it at three ecumenical conferences: 1901, in London; in 1911 in Toronto; and 1921 in London.[73]

Upon his return to the institution Atkins began to step up its curriculum by adding two years of standard normal work and by 1920 the first class completed the required course.[74]

In 1925 the charter of the institution was amended by Act of the North Carolina General Assembly and the name was changed to Winston-Salem Teachers College.

The enrollment in 1957-58 was 938; the approximate value of the institution's facilities, $4,500,000. Upon the death of Dr. Atkins, his son F. L. Atkins succeeded to the presidency. Under his able leadership the institution has made progress in the tradition of its eminent founder, S. G. Atkins.

Among the many graduates who have gone out from this institution, the following are representative of the fine work of the Atkins', the O'Kelleys' and many other consecrated workers, past and present who taught them. The list follows: Dr. R. S. Hairston, druggist, Winston-Salem, a Trustee of the institution, Dr. Marshall Shepard, former Register of Deeds, Washington, D. C.; Harvey Atkins, Deputy Clerk City Council, Cleveland, Ohio; Mrs. Juliette Bursterman, Associate Professor, State Teachers College, William-

---

72. Biennial Report State Superintendent Public Instruction 1894-96.

73. Newbold, North Carolina *Five Negro Educators*, p. 16.

74. *Ibid.*, p. 13.

antic, Connecticut; Mrs. Bessie D. Wilder, Supervisor of Schools, Halifax County; Mrs. T. C. Beam, Supervisor of Schools, Caswell County, Mrs. Nora Lockhart, Principal, Crosby-Garfield School, Raleigh; A. B. Reynolds, Principal, Columbia Heights Junior High School, Winston-Salem; and F. L. Atkins, President, State Teachers College, Winston-Salem.[75]

Agricultural and Technical College (Greensboro, N. C.)

The North Carolina Agricultural and Technical College, better known by its initials "A. and T. College" is the State's Negro counterpart of State College of Agriculture and Engineering as a "Land Grant" college.

In order to understand the term, "Land Grant," it is necessary to explain its origin. It began with the Morrill Act of 1862 which provided funds from the sale of western lands for the establishment of institutions in every state for the teaching of agriculture and mechanics. Since the funds granted came from land sales by the United States Government, the institutions were called "Land Grant" colleges. In the southern states the policy of separate schools for the Negroes necessitated two such institutions where the state could meet the provisions of the Morrill Act.

At the first the money derived from the land grant funds went to the University at Chapel Hill as it was not until 1887 that the Agricultural and Mechanical College (now State College of Agriculture and Engineering) was established at Raleigh. [76]

A. and T. College was organized March 9, 1891 as A. and M. College. Oddly enough, as State College got its start at the University, A. and T. was first an annex of Shaw University at Raleigh. John O. Crosby was its first administrator.[77]

The citizens of Greensboro wanted the institution located in that city and proceeded to secure lands for that purpose. One of the first citizens to whom they appealed for help was James William Scott of J. W. Scott and Company, who was always ready and willing to help Negroes in need.[78]

Fourteen acres of land was donated by friends of the project, $10,000 was appropriated by the General Assembly, and $11,000 was raised from local sources for the construction of a building which was completed in 1893 when the school was moved from Raleigh to Greensboro.

Under the second Morrill Act of 1890, the school became a land grant college for teaching agriculture and mechanic arts. Its gen-

---

75. Informationnaire—F. L. Atkins, President, Winston-Salem Teachers College.

76. Dabney, Charles Williams, *Universal Education in the South*, Vol. I, p. 188.

77. Informationnaire, W. T. Gibbs, President, A. and T. College.

78. Caldwell, Battie D., *Founders and Builders of Greensboro*, 1925, p. 323.

JAMES B. DUDLEY

President, A. and T. College
1896-1925

eral maintenance came from the State of North Carolina. Thus was the establishment of A. and T. College.[79]

Like the Fayetteville, Elizabeth City, and Winston-Salem institutions, the history of A. and T. centers around a great pioneer educator, James B. Dudley who served as its head from 1896 until his death in 1925.

Dudley had been a leader in the Farmers' Alliance movement and helped win the legislation that provided for the establishment of the institution. He had been president of the Teachers Association for six years and was appointed to the Board of Trustees of A. and T. by the State Legislature in 1895. Upon the resignation of John O. Crosby in 1896, he was appointed President of the college.[80]

The college was at first coeducational with domestic science being offered for women, but because of a lack of accommodation this was discontinued in 1900 and instruction became for males only. The courses offered in 1902 were agriculture, chemistry, and agricultural industries, brick-laying, brick-making, plastering, shoe making, tanning, harness making, heating and ventilating, repairs, and plumbing. The agricultural industries included dairying, horticulture, stock-raising, and general farm work.[81]

During the era of N. C. Newbold and the upsurge of teacher training the institution conducted the largest summer school for teachers in the state. Its director was F. D. Bluford, who succeeded to the presidency upon the death of Dudley in 1925.

Under the leadership of Bluford, A. and T. again became co-educational in 1926, and an era of phenomenal expansion began. The physical expansion is inextricably connected with the name of E. R. Hodgin, who came to A. and T. as Secretary-Treasurer in 1923. He is at present, (1959) the Business Manager. The name of Hodgin is inscribed on the plaques of practically every building on the campus.

During the governorship of R. Gregg Cherry the college received $2,000,000 through the State Legislature; while during the administration of Governor W. Kerr Scott, it received nearly $8,000,000 which brought about the greatest expansion since World War II. From this generous appropriation, several magnificent structures replaced the old army buildings known as "ORD" (now North Campus), acquired at the close of the war. Here is housed the "Technical Institute," a magnificent tribute to statesmanship of F. D. Bluford and the business sagacity of E. R. Hodgin.[82]

Further expansion and enlargement of the course of study came after World War II included a variety and specialization in education, sciences, graduate study and mili-

79. The Bulletin 1953, A. and T. College, p. 26, 27.

80. Newbold, N. C., *Five Negro Educators*, p. 42.

81. Biennial Report, State Superintendent Public Instruction, 1900-02, p. 434.

82. Information—E. R. Hodgin, Business Manager, August 1959.

tary training. Nothing is more indicative of this expansion than a comparison of the bulletin of the college in 1903, which contained only a few pages, with that of 1953-54, which contained several hundred pages. There are less tangible indexes of growth, which are not altogether unreliable in measurement of educational development, namely graduates. What kind of product are they? What is the nature of their services and the places they hold in the social order? Every county in the state where Negro families live and a great many outside—keep sending their children to A. and T. This fact is no doubt a great human tribute and sacrifice to the tide of good will generated by the college. *F. D. Bluford,* late President of the college.[83]

Bluford died December 21, 1955 after thirty years of service as President and was succeeded by W. T. Gibbs, who had served as Dean of the college.

The college was accepted into full membership by the Southern Association of Colleges and Secondary Schools at its annual meeting held in Louisville, Kentucky, December 4, 1959. The drive for accreditation had begun under the presidency of the late F. D. Bluford and accomplished by his successor, President W. T. Gibbs and the combined efforts of students, faculty, alumni, and friends all of whom had worked toward eradicating the inadequacies which had prevented an earlier accreditation.

As with other colleges reviewed in this work, it is difficult to list the many fine graduates who have gone out from the institution. Yet, the following must be mentioned: Clyde Donnell, long time medical examiner of the North Carolina Mutual Life Insurance Company; John W. Mitchell, United States regional Agricultural agent, Washington, D. C. (deceased); S. C. Smith, Dean of the Technical Institute of A. and T. College; S. B. Simmons, (deceased), North Carolina State Supervisor of vocational agriculture; Leon P. Miller, Attorney-General, Virgin Islands; and Dr. N. E. Patterson, medical doctor, Farrell, Pennsylvania.[84]

In 1960, Dr. Samuel D. Proctor, president of Virginia Union University, Richmond, Va., was elected to succeed Dr. W. T. Gibbs as president of A. and T. College.

North Carolina College at Durham

When Newbold authored the book, Five North Carolina Negro Educators in 1939, James E. Shepard was still living. Had that book been written after 1949, it most definitely would have included Shepard as a sixth North Carolina Negro educator for indeed he was all that the term can possibly imply.

---

83. Greensboro Daily News—June 26, 1955.

84. Informationnaire, W. T. Gibbs, President A. and T. College.

The objective of this story is to tell about the institution he founded and not the man for it remains for a truly great author, Helen E. Edmonds, Professor of History at North Carolina College, to write the life of James E. Shepard. However, in writing the history of the institution it is impossible to leave out the man, for he truly was "Mr. North Carolina College" himself.

Shepard started out in life as a politician and voted first in the Fusion Period of 1896. He was comparer of deeds in the office of H. P. Cheatham in 1898 and collector of customs in Raleigh in 1900 to 1905.[85] Although he had studied theology he graduated from the School of Pharmacy at Shaw University in 1894 and was one of the first Negro druggists in North Carolina. He was appointed Field Superintendent of Sunday School work by the Executive Committee of the International Sunday School Association and, while in this work, he was inspired to organize a school for religious training.

On land donated by white citizens in Durham on July 10, 1910, Shepard established the institution known as the National Religious Training School and Chatauqua. By April 1912 there were ten buildings valued at $125,000. Students came from several states and some from Africa and the West Indies.[86]

The purpose of the school was to develop in young men and young women fine character and sound academic training requisite for real service to the nation.[87]

In its first fifty years of existence, the institution experienced remarkable changes in development as well as in name. It was sold in 1915 and its name changed to The National Training School. In 1923, it became Durham State Normal School, thus increasing to four the number of normal schools in the state.

While Newbold was seeking to expand Slater Normal into a four-year teachers' college at Winston-Salem, Shepard induced the Legislature to convert Durham Normal into a college of liberal arts and for preparation of teachers and principals for the secondary schools. Thus the institution became the North Carolina College for Negroes. The sincere interest of Governor Angus W. McLean and generous contributions of B. N. Duke and other white friends in Durham inspired a remarkable expansion in facilities and in depth of curriculum.

Graduate work was adopted in 1939, a School of Law began operation in 1940, and the School of Library Science was established in 1941. The present name, North Carolina College at Durham, was adopted by Legislative act in 1947.

85. Edmonds, Helen E., *The Negro in Fusion Politics*, p. 92.

86. Whitted, J. A., *Biographical Sketch of Augustus Shepard*, pp. 20, 21.

87. Brown, Allen S., *Opportunities in Higher Education*, Unpublished Thesis, North Carolina College, p. 58.

JAMES E. SHEPARD, *Founder*
North Carolina College
Durham

Shepard died in 1947 and Alfonso Elder became president in 1948.[88]

The institution in 1958 had an enrollment of 1600 students and its total facilities were valued at $10,000,000.[89]

Aside from its able president, Alfonso Elder, the institution has been staffed by many highly trained educators who make the college an outstanding university, an enviable parallel to the State's university at Chapel Hill.

Some of the outstanding graduates of North Carolina College are: A. T. Spaulding, an insurance actuary and executive; L. E. Alston, newspaper editor; J. M. Hubbard, dentist and civic leader; R. L. McDougald (deceased), former banker and civic leader; H. M. Michaux, real estate operator; and James T. Taylor, professor of psychology at North Carolina College.[90]

88. North Carolina College Bulletin, 1958-1959, pp. 21, 23.

89. Informationnaire—Alphonse Elder, President North Carolina College at Durham.

90. *Ibid.*

Chapter VII

Special Secondary And Welfare Institutions

The institutions treated in this chapter are not to be considered in the same category although they are discussed in the same chapter. The first two are listed as "Special Secondary" because of their unique character of training which places them in a class by themselves apart from the collegiate institutions treated in another chapter.

Palmer Institute and Laurinburg Institute are the type of schools which early New Englanders might call "Finishing Schools." They make no pretense of performing college functions, for they are strictly secondary; yet they bear many resemblances to well ordered college campuses.

Both of these institutions have withstood the pressure of standardization in public education and have competed satisfactorily with the standards set in the public secondary schools.

The welfare institutions, except that of the Colored Orphanage, are properties of the state and are wholly maintained through appropriations of the State Legislature. The Colored Orphanage is maintained largely through efforts of the Masons and church groups. The correctional institutions are set up to meet the challenges of delinquency, but their chief activity is purely educational and must be thought of as such in attempting to correct social attitudes of children with which public schools had found it impossible to cope.

In the institutions for the blind and deaf, as well as in the mental institutions, the educational objective is more far reaching in that their aims are not only to keep their clientele from becoming public charges, but to aid them in living normal lives of happiness and usefulness.

Palmer Memorial Institute

The name Charlotte Hawkins Brown is practically synonymous with that of Palmer Memorial Institute because for more than a half century she guided the destiny of that institution.

Palmer was founded by Charlotte Hawkins Brown at Sedalia, N. C., in 1901 under the auspices of the American Missionary Association. She had been educated in the best of New England schools and learned how to make friends among the wealthy and influential.

Dr. Brown (she holds three honorary Doctor's degrees from outstanding colleges) was born in Henderson, N. C., but reared and educated in Massachusetts at Cambridge where she was fortunate to have the personal interest of the Charles W. Eliot family. Dr.

100

CHARLOTTE HAWKINS BROWN
Founder
Palmer Memorial Institute, Sedalia

Eliot, Harvard's president for fifty years, was first chairman of the board of trustees at Palmer Institute.

The school was originally located in a little white church four miles from McLeansville, "a little whistle stop," on the Southern Railroad. Later moving the school to Sedalia, she secured a United States post office largely for the use of the school.[1]

Schooled in the social graces, Dr. Brown sought to instill high qualities of culture in her students. Said the Greensboro Daily News, Sunday July 8, 1951, "Among the educational aims are two outstanding ones: to teach the dignity of labor, the emphasis of politeness and general culture." Palmer students walk through hallways, always alert to the signs overhead which read "Move quietly—Speak Softly; and the expressions 'Thank You' and 'If You Please' are bywords."[2]

The institution has maintained a high secondary school standard and accepts only picked students with high standards in their communities. They have come even from far away Africa, so widely has the reputation of Palmer spread.

When a girls' dormitory burned in mid winter of 1950, the school not only continued uninterruptedly, but through the beneficence of white and Negro friends, North as well as South, replaced the dormitory within eight months.

On the 459 acres owned by the school, Dr. Brown taught the students to farm scientifically and started the first vocational department for Negroes in the state.

Said the late S. B. Simmons, Supervisor of Vocational Agriculture in North Carolina, "These boys not only have farmed with profit to the school and themselves, but they have proved to those who may have doubts that school farms can be made to pay, that scientific and practical farming can be combined with profit."[3]

Dr. Brown retired in 1952 and was succeeded by Wilhelmina Crosson, of Boston, Massachusetts, who had served as her assistant.

Laurinburg Institute

One of the few Church-supported secondary schools to survive the Newbold era is the Laurinburg Institute, located in the town of Laurinburg. Roanoke Institute of Elizabeth City is the only other church-supported secondary school which did not turn its property over to the state during the period of standardization of Negro secondary schools. However, this institution has existed for the most part as a school for ministers.

Laurinburg Institute, however, has maintained its property and also its standard as a well organized private secondary school.

---

1. Tone—a reprint—National Magazine, February 1952, p. 2.

2. Greensboro Daily News, Greensboro, N. C., July 8, 1951.

3. Isaac J. Johnson, "Pattern for Living," Message Magazine, June 1953.

It was founded by Emmanuel Montee McDuffie, a Baptist minister, who was born in Snow Hill, Alabama, and educated at the Snow Hill Institute and Tuskegee Institute, where he was a pupil of Booker T. Washington. He established the Laurinburg Normal and Industrial Institute at Laurinburg in Scotland County in 1904. He was deeply imbued with the idea of Negroes having something for themselves and, as an apostle of Booker Washington's philosophy, he knew that education was the one way out for his race. He took children into his school at whatever standard they had attained and taught them what they could learn.

The institution started with one teacher and four students, but grew with the years to be the only opportunity for secondary training for the Negro in Scotland County. Today, with a public high school within sight of the institute, the school is still operating at full strength. Not only did it offer facilities to the boys and girls who came from outside the county, up to 1952 it gave freely without any compensation from state, county, or local government the use of its facilities and equipment for operating the only public school system for Negro students in Scotland County.

The school is located within the town limits of Laurinburg. Its campus contains about ten buildings and several teachers' cottages, including a boys' dormitory, a girls' dormitory, administration building, a home economics building, a gymnasium, an auto-mechanics building, and a vocational shop. New construction had started in 1959 to replace old buildings with modern structures including a new dormitory for boys, one for girls, a cafeteria, and a new classroom building with business and administrative offices.

The grounds provide space for a large truck garden which produces much of the food consumed by the staff and students.

The institution provides adequate religious, social, athletic and other activities. All students are required to attend Sunday School on the campus, but may attend a church of their choice in the city. In athletics the institution boasts of several achievements. In 1951, its basketball team was recognized as the nation's number one high school team. The 1954 team won the National High School Basketball championship game played at Tennessee State University in Nashville. Wes Covington, who plays with the Milwaukee Braves' baseball team, and Sam Jones, who plays with the Boston Celtics basketball team, both received most of their training at Laurinburg Institute.

The institution was chartered in 1906 and, while its curriculum is strictly secondary, it retains its name, Laurinburg Institute.

McDuffie died in 1953 and was succeeded by his son, Frank McDuffie, who was educated at Hampton Institute, A & T College, and holds a Master's degree from the University of Pittsburgh.

Some outstanding graduates of Laurinburg are: Dr. Leo L. Oxley, 1953, third ranking in his class at Meharry Medical College, Nashville; Dr. Kenneth Chambers, First Honor graduate of Laurinburg Institute in 1952; James Golden, a graduate of Winston-Salem

Teachers College, now a successful coach at Carver High School, Laurel Hill, S. C.; John Russell, a graduate of North Carolina College, now coaching at Red Springs; and Anzell Harrell, a graduate of North Carolina College, now a band director at Shaw High School, Wagram, N. C.

That this institution has been maintained with such a creditable standard is a tribute to the ingenuity of its founder, Emmanuel McDuffie, his widow, Mrs. McDuffie, who in her declining years is still an inspiration on the campus, and to their son, Frank McDuffie, who is following in his father's footsteps.[4]

The Colored Orphanage at Oxford

Augustus Shepard, father of the founder of North Carolina College, Durham, N. C., is largely credited with the beginnings of the Colored Orphanage at Oxford. However, it resulted from activities of Baptist associations, Shiloh and Wake.

Shepard, a Baptist minister, had travelled over the state and had seen large numbers of homeless, neglected children. A powerful and dramatic speaker (I heard him speak on his journeys in Africa while I was a student at Hampton Institute) he doubtless made a deep impression upon his fellow ministers of various Baptist Associations. As a result the Colored Orphanage Association was formed in August, 1882.

In October, 1883 a farm of twenty-three acres located one and one-half miles from Oxford was obtained for $1,565 and the orphanage named "Grant Colored Orphanage." The name was changed in 1887 to Colored Orphanage Asylum of North Carolina.

The first superintendent of "Grant Orphanage" was the Reverend Joshua Perry, who served one year, and was succeeded by a Canadian woman, Miss Bessie Hockin, who served without salary from 1884 to 1886. She not only served without salary, but also donated to the Orphanage her furniture. During that time, one Henry Hester, of Oxford, volunteered to pay all bills contracted in providing food for the orphans and served as treasurer until his death in 1901.

Additional land, forty-four acres, was purchased in 1895 for $1,440; four years later in 1898 another acre was bought; it was located directly opposite the orphanage, and on it a home for the superintendent was erected. There was a later addition of three acres on which was located a well built house and on Thanksgiving Day 1903, twenty young children and a matron moved into this new home.

Donations from white friends, churches, fraternal orders and even from the State Legislature assured the continuance of the institution.

H. P. Cheatham, ex-congressman, served as superintendent from 1907 to 1935. During his long tenure, the old frame buildings were

---

4. Bulletin—Laurinburg Institute, 1959-60.

replaced with brick structures. The bricks were made on the orphanage grounds by the boys of the orphanage. The Angier B. Duke school and office building was erected as a gift of B. N. Duke. The farm acreage during the Cheatham era increased to 400 acres.

Cheatham died in 1935 and was succeeded by his son, Charles, who served for two years. He was succeeded in 1937 by T. K. Borders, during whose administration a heating plant was installed and a sewer system was connected with the town of Oxford.

Succeeding superintendents include C. A. Alston, 1940 to 1941; T. A. Hamme, 1941 to 1951 and the present incumbent, T. H. Brooks.

The institution is continuing to expand its facilities in the effort to meet the ever increasing need for its service in keeping with present day needs. Today the plant and campus bear the appearance of a well-kept small college site.[5]

North Carolina State School for the Blind and Deaf

First attention to the education of the Negro deaf and dumb and the Negro blind in North Carolina was given by the State in 1867.

The Federal Government assisted by paying rent and supplying rations. A school was opened January 4, 1869, in a building rented from The American Missionary Association in the southeastern part of Raleigh. The original enrollment included twenty-one deaf and seven blind pupils.

By 1873 the State began to assume more responsibility for the program by appropriating five thousand dollars for a building erected on South Bloodworth Street in Raleigh. The building was occupied in the summer of 1874. A wing was added in 1897 when the State's annual appropriation had increased from $40,000 to $72,500. In addition to this wing, an industrial building and a three-story dormitory for the boys was built.

William J. Young taught vocational training at the school for twenty years and served as principal from 1883 to 1896. During his tenure the enrollment increased to ninety students.

The name of the institution was changed in 1905 from "The North Carolina Institution for the Instruction of the Negro Blind, Deaf and Dumb" to the simpler name, "State School for the Blind and Deaf," the term, dumb, was eliminated from the name of the school because it was discovered that even though a person may be deaf, he may still have speech.

The institution was moved in 1931 to its present site on the old U. S. Route 70, two and a half miles southeast of Raleigh. This was made possible by an appropriation of $250,000 by the 1929 General Assembly.

Since 1945 two new dormitories, a home for the principal, a gymnasium, a classroom building and an auditorium have been built.

5. Report of Board of Directors, Oxford Colored Orphanage, 1959. Interview, T. H. Brooks, Superintendent.

During the 1959-60 school term a vocational building and expansion of dining-room and dormitories to provide recreational facilities were under construction.

Through the expert training of instructors, students are educated to become self-sufficient citizens. Many of them marry, rear families, and enjoy home life. Of the eight graduates from the Blind Department who have completed college degrees, four are now teaching at the State School For the Deaf and Blind; one is a band major of A & T College, another connected with the North Carolina Mutual Life Insurance Company; one deaf student has finished college at Gallaudet, Washington, D. C.

The original and subsequent heads of the institution are: Frank Debnam, William J. Young, John E. Ray, G. E. Lineberry, Egbert N. Peeler, Charlie Williams, D. A. W. Pegues, the Reverend A. B. Johnson, the Reverend M. W. Williams, J. W. Mask, J. T. Turner, and M. H. Crockett.

The professional personnel in 1958 included a superintendent, a principal, twenty-seven academic teachers, eleven vocational teachers, one physical education teacher, one recreational teacher, one guidance counsellor, one librarian and two part-time librarians.

The institution is entirely state supported.[6]

Morrison Training School

"Save a Boy" was a movement started in 1915 in Charlotte to meet the challenge of juvenile delinquency. Judge Heriot Clarkson, later to become a State Supreme Court Justice, and Thaddeus L. Tate, a Negro Social worker, both of Charlotte, were pioneers in the movement for Negro boys.

A small building was erected on a tract of land purchased through private donations, but proved wholly inadequate.

In 1921, a bill to establish a correctional school for Negro boys was passed by the General Assembly, and $21,000 was appropriated, but lack of proper earmarking dissipated the appropriation into other purposes. The General Assembly of 1923 appropriated $50,-000 specifically for a training school for delinquent Negro boys.

In 1924 a tract of land containing 400 acres was purchased in Richmond County, birthplace of Cameron Morrison, Governor of the State at the time and in honor of him, the school was named "Morrison Training School." The first building erected was named Varser Hall in honor of Judge Varser, who cleared the land titles.

The school opened January 5, 1925 with the Reverend L. Boyd as superintendent; he served until March 1, 1944, when he was succeeded by P. R. Brown, the present head of the institution.

The site now numbers over seven hundred acres, of which over three hundred are under cultivation. More than four hundred boys were under institutional care in 1959.

6. M. H. Crockett, *A Brief History of North Carolina State School for the Blind and Deaf*, 1958.

The staff members number seventy-six. The approximate value of the facilities in June, 1958 was $1,178,329.

Many students return to their communities completely rehabilitated and become worthwhile citizens.[7]

EDUCATION OF MENTAL DEFECTIVES

State Asylum (Now Cherry Hospital)

Education in general is usually thought of as "The training of individuals for life activities." Few people ever consider the care of mental patients as an educational function any more than they would the temporary treatment of an individual in a regular hospital. However, no history of the education of Negroes in North Carolina (or of whites, for that matter) can justly ignore the wonderful work which mental institutions have done toward mental restoration of those whose minds had gone astray. A broader view of education has come to mean something more than merely training for life activities, but a restoration of those whose minds might be restored to normal activities.

Before man had progressed far enough in his thinking to provide any sort of public care for mental defectives, a lunatic might be shut up in a dark room or even chained to keep him from inflicting bodily injury to himself or to others. An imbecile might be merely shunned; no one knowing how or thinking about improving his plight or sharing with him any of life's blessings except food and clothing. True enough, many Christian-hearted people had sympathy for these unfortunates, but knew little or nothing about meeting the problem.

The fact that the first institutions were called "asylums" indicates the feeling of sympathy toward providing a "retreat or rest," not a treatment for such unfortunates.

In North Carolina the need for mental care of Negro mental defectives was felt long before any scientific action was taken to provide treatment of mental diseases. As far back as 1872, legislative reports show that reimbursements were made to various counties for each "lunatic" who had been adjudged as such by two respectable physicians..

Prior to 1880, some Negroes had been cared for at the insane asylum in Raleigh and also at a Marine Hospital in Wilmington. In 1874 the General Assembly appropriated $20,000 for support of the colored insane and also $10,000 per annum toward the establishment of a branch at the Marine Hospital building in Wilmington.

A joint committee of the Senate and the House of the General Assembly was appointed to select a site for the colored insane at some point in the State and for the support and maintenance of the inmates thereof for the following two years. Governor Zebulon B. Vance was authorized to appoint seven commissioners whose

---

7. Report of Paul R. Brown, Superintendent, Morrison Training School, 1959.

duty was to locate said asylum and to procure suitable buildings either by purchase, donation or by superintendency of erection as in their judgment might be deemed most expedient.

On April 11, 1878, the commissioners purchased from William T. Dortch and wife 170.97 acres of land two miles west of Goldsboro for the sum of $5,000. The contract for the first building was let at a cost of $22,700. One year later, the sum of $20,000 was appropriated for further construction and the asylum was opened August 1, 1880.

By the end of 1880, there were 91 patients who filled the building to its capacity. It was estimated that from 75 to 100 colored insane in various parts of the state still remained to be cared for. The fact that in March, 1881, the sum of $15,500 per annum in addition to the initital establishment of the institution was appropriated is proof positive that the Christian philosophy, "The strong must bear the infirmities of the weak," had been accepted by the Christian people of the state.

Eastern North Carolina Insane Asylum

On March 5, 1881, the Asylum was constituted a corporation and designated, The Eastern North Carolina Insane Asylum. The affairs of the Corporation would be managed by a board of nine directors, of which a quorum of five would manage its business and make all necessary by-laws governing the institution. They would serve without remuneration except for their traveling expenses incurred in the discharge of their official duties. The by-laws and reports of the Superintendent and treasurer were to be published with their reports to the General Assembly.

Buildings

The development of the physical facilities over the years has been remarkable. A superintendent's home was erected in 1884. By 1889, telephone connection with Goldsboro was installed. The following year electric lights were provided to replace an ineffective gas machine lighting system; during the summer of 1889, the old gas machine broke down and for over a month, the wards were in darkness except for "lard burners." Tenement houses were erected and bath rooms installed and a hot blast system of heating was provided. A brick yard plant was built to provide building materials.

By 1902 electric call bells for the main office, an electric fire alarm, and outside electric lights had been installed. By 1920, the facilities had expanded to accommodate 1,530 patients. By 1930, the entire plant practically had been rebuilt and, with aid from the P.W.A. (Public Works Administration) an extensive building program had made the institution one of the finest of its kind any where. In 1960 there were eight buildings accommodating thirteen hundred female patients and seven buildings accommodating fifteen hundred and seventy male. In addition there is an Occupational Therapy building containing shops, sewing rooms, and a canteen. A chapel with a seating capacity of 600 was completed in 1950. It contains a recreational hall with various exercise equipment. In this chapel, appropriate moving pictures and other means of entertainment are provided as a part of the educational practice of the institution.

Other buildings include a staff house erected in 1940, a nurses' home, a new kitchen, cafeteria, and diet kitchen completed in 1959; a warehouse or storage building, completed in 1930; a new water plant in 1952; a superintendent's residence, a business manager's residence, 64 single housing units, 55 duplex units all of which house institution employees.

For many years, the institution was known by the simple name, State Hospital, but in 1959, its name was changed to "Cherry Hospital" in honor of the late Governor R. Gregg Cherry. The approximate value of the institution's facilities in 1960 was 24 million dollars; it covers more than 3,435 acres of land; it employs more than 600 persons, of whom more than 400 are Negro; it contains a patient population of more than 3,000. The surrounding area is a veritable "college-like" community. Its residents seem to speak proudly, "I live out at the State (now Cherry)."

Progress of Treatment

Before the era of scientific treatment, there appeared little hope for patients being restored to normal living. True there were many discharges and some appeared completely restored in mind, but most of the treatment was said to be no more than hospital care. To the layman, a mental breakdown seemed one of hopelessness. There was always the long waiting list. Today it has been completely abolished. Before 1956, only 4 per cent received any psychiatric treatment; there was no psychiatric therapy; there were no tranquilizing drugs. Now with admissions up to 1500 per year, discharges are even higher. In 1959-60 there were 1,500 admitted and 1,600 discharged.

The medical and surgical services include clinical directors, staff physicians, surgeons, dentists, psychologists, laboratory technicians, pharmacists, all type nurses, social service, occupational therapy, and religious activities. The entire work of the institution is truly an educational challenge and bravely and efficiently has the State risen to meet it.

Personnel

The first superintendent of the institution was Dr. William Moore. The following have succeeded him: Dr. J. D. Roberts, Dr. J. F. Miller, Dr. W. W. Faison, who worked for 40 years at the institution and served 21 years as superintendent until his death in 1926; Dr. W. C. Linville, Dr. F. L. Whelpley, Dr. Ira Long, and the present incumbent, Dr. M. M. Vitolls.

Dr. Vitolls, a native of Latvia, was educated at the University of Hamburg in Germany and at the University of North Carolina. He took charge of the institution in 1956. The institution had, in 1956, its first business manager, Roy M. Purser, who served until 1959, when he was succeeded by J. W. Gaddy, who was still in office in 1960.

Among the early Negro employees who seemed to act with authority and who were held in high esteem among patients and administrators are: Arnold Howell, Joshua Howell (who was still living in 1960), and Mrs. Cora Mitchell, all known as attendants. Albert Whitaker, who came to the institution in 1923 and who has served the institution for thirty-seven years, is now supervisor of attendants.

Before the chapel was built and a chaplain employed, religious services were conducted voluntarily. Among those who served in this capacity were the Reverends C. A. Reid, David A. Baker and J. J. Tillett. The first chaplain was the Reverend J. S. Brown, who was succeeded by the Reverend R. M. Coley.

Other Negroes in a professional status are: Gene A. Bass, psychologist, Mrs. Ruth McKeithian and Mrs. Rowenna Barnes, social workers, and Mrs. Dorothy Lambert and Mrs. Irene Allen, Registered Nurses.[8]

State Training School For Girls

Even though somewhat belated, the State deserves great credit for its efforts in meeting the challenge of delinquency among its Negro youth. Yet it must be said that greater commendation is due an interested group of dedicated women, led by Charlotte Hawkins Brown, who made the first attempt to establish an institution to cope with the vexing problem of delinquency among girls.

Through the State Federation of Colored Women's Clubs, she kept the cause of wayward girls constantly before the State Legislature and the entire people of the state. They could not wait for the Legislature to make up its mind over a period of several legislatures, but launched out upon their own faith and limited finances to set up an institution known as Efland Home on old Highway 10 between Hillsboro and Graham.

It was in 1928 when the home was opened by the Woman's Federation and through the efforts of club women and some contributions from white friends, the institution struggled on until 1943 when lack of funds to maintain it forced it to close. By that time, the Legislature had made up its mind and appropriated $50,000 for the establishment of a "Training School" for delinquent Negro girls. The first location was on the site and in the buildings used

---

8. History of State (Cherry) Hospital, prepared for Goldsboro News Argus, 1960, by George Slaymaker and Eunice McCullough.
Interviews: Dr. M. M. Vitolls, Superintendent; J. W. Gaddy, Business Manager; The Reverend R. M. Coley, Chaplain.

by the old N. Y. A. at Rocky Mount. The institution was opened with appropriate ceremonies on September 12, 1944 featuring Governor J. Melville Broughton, Dr. Charlotte Hawkins Brown, and Dr. Ellen Winston, Superintendent of the State Welfare Department.

The institution was moved from Rocky Mount to Dobbs Farm, near Kinston on July 1, 1947. This site had formerly been used as a detention home for white delinquents and was considerably more spacious than the old N. Y. A. buildings. Considerable improvements have been made including four modern brick buildings, and two others under construction in 1960.

The personnel includes 28 full time and five part time workers. There are a superintendent, budget officer, educational director, regular teachers, food service personnel, house counsellors, social workers, religious educational workers, farmer, nurse, and physician. The number of students in 1959-60 was 110.

The type of training is essentially that found in most any public school although vocational and religious education is emphasized. Every effort is made to rehabilitate the students into moral and normal living. The administrative head is Miss Mae D. Holmes, who started with the establishment of the institution as its Superintendent. Others include Miss Ethel Parker, Secretary; James R. Covington Sr., Budget Officer; Miss Laura L. Edwards, Religious Education Director; and B. M. Madison, Commissioner of Correction and Training.[9]

O'BERRY SCHOOL—Training of the Mentally Retarded

The problem of the care and/or the training of mentally retarded children had plagued school officials and communities for many years before the public mind awakened to a sense of its duty toward a proper approach to cope with the problem so far as colored mentally retarded were concerned. A school for the white mentally retarded had been established many years before any effort to establish one for Negroes was considered. Mentally retarded Negro children were either kept at home, placed in the public schools or, when adjudged a menace to society, were confined in "colonies" at the State Hospital for the insane and given custodial care only.

It is to the eternal credit of the late Thomas O'Berry, State Senator, of Goldsboro, and Representative John Umstead, of Chapel Hill, that North Carolina moved to meet the challenging problem of the mentally retarded colored children. It was in 1945 that the State Legislature, upon the insistence of Senator O'Berry, authorized the establishment of a school for the mentally retarded colored children to be located on the lands of the State Hospital. However, it was not until 1955 that an appropriation was made for the

---

9. Interview: Miss Mae D. Holmes, Superintendent, State Training School for Girls.

construction of a building. A bevy of buildings soon sprang up and in September, 1957, the institution was opened to about 100 mentally retarded children who had been incarcerated in the "colony" at the State Hospital.

The school is situated on a site of approximately 55 acres, west of, but in close proximity to Cherry Hospital. However, the institution is a distinct entity and officially disconnected from Cherry Hospital. There were in 1960 ten cottages, an administration building, a multi-purpose facility, an infirmary, a non-ambulatory hospital for crippled children, a staff house, a kitchen, and a cafeteria. A projected million dollar hospital building is in prospect as a part of the state-wide bond issue voted in 1958. The approximate value of all facilities of the institution is four million dollars; the appropriation for maintenance in 1959-60 was $825,000.

Concerning the objectives of the school, the intent is to provide training for all who can be trained; custodial care for those not able to be trained; separation of the educable from the non-educable. Rehabilitation is slow; efforts in that direction are being made.

The enrollment in 1960 was up to 600. Children are admitted between the ages of 6 and 20. If the national average that three out of every 100 births will be mentally retarded, the enrollment will double in the next ten years.

The institution in 1960 had a personnel of 150 employees of which 135 were Negroes. With a present waiting list of 400, the number of employees may conceivably go much higher. The main officials of the institution are: the superintendent, Dr. Vernon Mangum; Business Manager, Roscoe Daniels; Director of Cottage Life, Andrew Holmes; Supervisor of Nurses, Mrs. Betty James; Chaplain, the Reverend J. E. Arnett; Dentist, Dr. R. M. Bell; Director of Training, William Waters; Principal, Thomas McNeil, and Ruby Whitted, Head Nurse Crippled Children's Cottage.

The school was named O'Berry School, in honor of the State Senator, the late Thomas O'Berry, of Goldsboro, who was instrumental in its establishment. John Umstead, of Chapel Hill, Chairman of the State Hospital's Board of Control, has been intensely interested in the development and maintenance of the institution.[10]

10. Interviews: Dr. Vernon Mangum, Superintendent O'Berry School; The Reverend J. E. Arnette, Chaplain; Roscoe Daniels, Business Manager.

Chapter VIII

Contingent Educational Influences

The North Carolina Teachers Association; the Extension Service; Nurse Education

The North Carolina Teachers Association

The Negro teachers who organized the first professional association were sensitive to the use of the word "Negro" in the association's name and preferred not to have it labeled "North Carolina Negro Teachers Association." It was finally agreed that since the white association was styled "North Carolina Teachers Assembly" (now North Carolina Education Association) the word "Negro" was not needed as a distinguishing mark and might be omitted.

The General Assembly, therefore, chartered the group as the "North Carolina Teachers Association" and the name has been retained to the present time.[1]

No people can ever run away from their origin, however humble it may be. Neither need they be ashamed of it whatever stigma might be attached by others.

> "Honor and shame from no condition rise; act well your
> part, there all the honor lies." (Pope)

That the Negro teachers have acted well their part in the professional game of education is shown in the story of this chapter.

No study of the education of the Negro in North Carolina could be complete without chronicling the annals of the North Carolina Teachers Association, the growth and influence of which have been phenomenal in the seventy-five years of its existence.

Early in the period of reconstruction, the pioneers of the Association conceived and recognized the importance of professional activity to bolster the educational efforts of teachers, for we quote from an essay by O. Hunter, Jr., Esq., a Negro teacher who addressed the Second Annual Convention of the North Carolina Educational Association on July 9, 1874.

A portion of Hunter's essay is quoted exactly as written:

> My observation and experience have taught one that a
> large number of different studies imposed upon the mind
> of the scholar, during any stage of his or her course of
> instruction, whether in the primary, academic, or collegiate
> department, is more of a determent to his or her progress
> than an auxiliary. When a person's mind is taxed with a
> multitude of a variety of different subjects, it is a matter
> of utter impossibility for that person to give that atten-

---

1. Official program, Sixty-first Annual Convention, North Carolina Teachers Association, Winston-Salem, April, 1942, p. 9.

ion to each which peradventure it may demand.

With the multiplicity of courses and "frills" which have crept into the modern curriculum, present day educators would say that Hunter was ahead of his time. Hunter also condemned the teaching of "defunct" languages (to use his term) instead of mother tongue. Continuing the essay, he wrote:

> I would not be afraid to risk the assertion that nine tenths of the schools in our state today teaching Latin, French, Greek (sic) and geometry where, if justice were done the student, they would, in lieu of teaching physiology, (sic) astronomy (especially since the appearance of the comet) practical and mental arithmetic.

The address was praised by S. S. Satchwell, C. H. Wiley and by General W. R. Cox, three of the most talented gentlemen in the convention.

Other colored men listed as being in the North Carolina Education Association were William Warrick, Caesar Johnson, and Robert Harris. Johnson was on the faculty of Shaw University.[2]

The Association had its beginning in the Hall of the House of Representatives in Raleigh in 1881, so said Dr. S. G. Atkins, one of its founders, speaking from the stage of Dillard High School in Goldsboro at the 1927 Convention.[3] Atkins mentioned the names of R. H. W. Leak, Bennett Goins, and John R. Hawkins as early leaders.

Although he did not mention Bishop J. W. Hood, it is most likely that Hood was among them, having been assistant superintendent of Public Instruction. Certainly Bishop Hood was living at the time for he published a book, "One Hundred Years of the A. M. E Zion Church," in 1895.[4]

At the 50th Anniversary, Golden Jubilee Convention, held at Winston-Salem in 1931, Dr. G. E. Davis, President at the time extolled the names of the pioneers of the Association as he delivered his masterful president's address. Said he on that memorable occasion:

> Common gratitude and love alike would dictate at least the calling of the names of these good men and women who thus suffered to produce the pioneer men and women of this Association. We owe them a debt we can never repay.

Davis then listed O. Hunter of Saint Augustine's, Tupper of Shaw, Steele of Bennett, Luke Dorland of Scotia, Matoon and Law-

---

2. Superintendents' Correspondence (Miscellaneous Negro Schools) State Department Archives, Raleigh.

3. N. C. Newbold, *Five North Carolina Negro Educators*, p. 19. Irma Todd, *History of the Development of The North Carolina Teachers Association*, Unpublished thesis, A. and T. College, 1952, pp. 7, 8.

4. W. J. (Bishop) Walls, *Joseph Charles Price; Educator and Race Leader*, 1943, p. 540.

rence of Biddle.

Among those who followed them Davis extolled as having made great contributions in building upon the foundation laid by the pioneers. He listed C. S. Brown of Winton, E. E. Smith of Fayetteville, G. C. Shaw of Oxford, John A. Savage of Albion Academy, Charlotte Hawkins Brown of Palmer, J. C. Price of Livingstone, S. G. Atkins of Winston-Salem, James E. Shepard of Durham, N. F. Roberts of Shaw, C. G. O'Kelley of Kittrell, D. J. Sanders of Biddle, T. S. Inborden of Bricks and P. W Moore of Elizabeth City.[5]

Place of Meetings

For the first decade of the Association, its annual meetings were held in the city of Raleigh, after which it moved to Kittrell College in Vance County for some eight or nine meetings. Aside from the fact that Kittrell was the site of an institution of higher learning the presence of its mineral springs was an added attraction and since the conventions were held for two weeks during the month of June, the teachers not only were inspired by the Association, but were given an opportunity to relax at a resort.

Near the turn of the century Dr. Henry Martin Tupper, President of Shaw University, invited the Association to meet as guests of Shaw. To encourage their acceptance he offered free entertainment and with the acceptance of this invitation, the Association began to rotate among the institutions and cities.[6]

Time of Meeting Changes

Since the meetings were held in June and summer schools were developing and as many teachers found it impossible to attend, the time was changed to Thanksgiving season for a two-day session. Prior to this change, membership and attendance barely reached two hundred.

The great spurt came in 1922 when Dr. S. G. Atkins, President of Winston-Salem State Normal invited the Association to Winston-Salem. The response was far beyond his most ardent hopes or expectations for, aside from having to feed his guests, Atkins had also obligated himself to lodge them for the two nights of the convention.

Although more than twice the expected number reported, Atkins magnificently rose to the occasion. There were not beds nor rooms enough, but friendly firms, most of whom had closed for the night, answered Dr. Atkins' call for cots, mattresses, and other bedding. One company completely exhausted its supply, but the situation was taken care of adequately, thanks to the fine inter-racial spirit existing in Winston-Salem. More than eight hundred teachers were in attendance at this convention and each succeeding year added new members.

---

5. North Carolina Teachers Record, May 1931, p. 44.

6. Official Program, *Op. cit.*, p. 9.

Leaders During the 20's

Dr. James E. Shepard was president during most of the period of the early 20's until a new constitution limited the term of the president. It was during the convention of 1926 at Livingstone College Dr. S. G. Atkins was elected president. Other leaders were W. A. Robinson, corresponding secretary and J. A. McRae, recording secretary.

The last Thanksgiving season meeting was held in Goldsboro in 1927 when the time was changed to the Easter season. No meeting was held in 1928.

It was at the Goldsboro convention in 1927 that Atkins made his memorable address reciting the early history of the Association. It was also at the Goldsboro convention that J. W. Seabrook, who had become corresponding secretary, proposed a full time secretary and the publication of a journal.

The following committee to investigate the possibility was appointed: W. S. Turner, H. V. Brown, O. R. Pope, F. G. Rogers, and P. W. Moore. This committee reported favorably at the Charlotte convention in 1929 and the proposal was adopted. L. S. Cozart was appointed Executive Secretary, and the journal, The North Carolina Teachers Record, made its first appearance January, 1930.[7] Concerning the publishing of the North Carolina Teachers Record, A. T. Allen, State Superintendent of Public Instruction had this to say:

> I am very much gratified that this Association has found
> it possible to publish a magazine of its own and I bespeak
> for it the hearty and undivided support of the state.[8]

Earlier in the history of the Association a journal called "The Progressive Educator" had been published and edited at various times by C. N. Hunter, S. G. Atkins, and C. H. Moore. This early publication was regarded by competent judges as one of North Carolina's best journalistic ventures.[9]

The present journal is the official organ of the Association and has been published in January, March, May, and October each year since its establishment in 1932. The Executive Secretary is also Editor of the journal. Sample copies up to the current year have been neatly bound and filed at the Headquarters building and represent a valuable reservoir of source material in the activities of the North Carolina Teachers Association .

Executive Secretary

Prior to 1930 the conduct of the business of the Association was more or less voluntary; being done on a part time basis without

---

7. North Carolina Teachers Record, January 1930, pp. 10, 13.

8. *Ibid.*, p. 9.

9. N. C. Newbld, *Op. cit.*, p. 20.

remuneration, by agents or officials in other functions. For several years W. A. Robinson as State Inspector of high schools and J W. Seabrook, Dean of Fayetteville State Normal, served as corresponding secretary. A nominal sum for correspondence and travel was permitted by a budget of one dollar per member. Prior to 1922 that amounted to approximately two hundred dollars annually. At Winston-Salem in 1922 the membership vaulted to 900.

As aforestated in 1929 at the Charlotte convention, J. W. Seabrook, then Corresponding Secretary, proposed a full time paid secretary which was adopted and activated in 1930. The budget at that time, covering the period from November, 1927 to March, 1929 (there being no meeting in 1928 due to change in time of meeting) was $2,550 with an actual expenditure of $2,342.39 leaving a balance of $207.61.[10]

It was upon this balance and the following school term expectancy in dues at $1.50 per member that the Executive Secretary program was started.[11]

L. S. Cozart was the first Executive Secretary and served from 1930 to 1932 when he resigned to become Dean of Barber-Scotia. G. E. Davis, who was completing his term as President, succeeded Cozart and served until 1943 when he retired. W. L. Greene succeeded Davis and has served with distinction up to the time of this recording.

Expansion

No one can more thoroughly appreciate the expansion of the North Carolina Teachers Association than the author of this book. With no attempt at egotism, he has been referred to as the "Father of the Districts," because of his long fight for and the final successful setting up of the original four district Associations.

W. A. Robinson, retired High School Inspector and formerly Corresponding Secretary of the Association, made the first suggestion for organizing districts at the Winston-Salem convention in 1922. The proposal was branded by Charlotte Hawkins Brown as an attempt to bring politics into the Association and the proposal died, or so it seemed, but the suggestion had made its impression which later would be a perennial "thorn in the flesh" of the Association's agenda.

The growth of the Association each year indicated a need for a closer look at its ability to function. Hardly an institution had an auditorium of sufficient size to accommodate the increasing numbers attending each year.

The second suggestion to propose a setting up of districts came to the writer from J. H. Carney returning from the Elizabeth City convention in 1932, ten years after the Robinson proposal at Winston-Salem. He suggested that the Association could better serve

10. North Carolina Teachers Record, January 1930, p. 21.
11. *Ibid.*, p. 10.

the teachers if it were divided into convenient districts. The proposal was made to the Convention of 1933 and again in 1934 only to be defeated at each convention.

A plan to provide for 13 districts was published by H. V. Brown in the January 1935 issue of the Teachers Record.[12] The plan also provided for a system of delegates from local units over the state. Brown kept his proposal before each convention until a final adoption of a four-district plan at the Charlotte Convention in 1936.

Charlotte Hawkins Brown who had denounced the proposal by Robinson in 1922, was President of the Association in 1936 and was not only in favor of the plan, but appointed H. V. Brown as State Organizer to put the plan into action. Thus after fourteen years of nursing the idea of W. A. Robinson, Brown took the North Carolina Teachers Association to the four corners of the state. If he was the "Father," certainly W. A. Robinson was the "Grandfather" of the districts.

The Original Four Districts

THE SOUTHEASTERN was composed of the following counties: Bladen, Brunswick, Carteret, Columbus, Craven, Cumberland, Duplin, Green, Harnett, Hoke, Jones, Lenoir, New Hanover, Onslow, Pamlico, Pender, Robeson, Sampson and Wayne.

THE NORTHEASTERN: Beaufort, Bertie Camden, Chowan, Currituck, Dare, Edgecombe, Gates, Halifax, Hertford, Hyde, Johnston, Martin, Nash, Northampton, Pasquotank, Perquimans, Pitt, Tyrrell, Washington and Wilson.

THE PIEDMONT: Alamance, Caswell, Chatham, Durham, Franklin, Granville, Guilford, Lee, Moore, Orange, Person, Randolph, Richmond, Rockingham, Scotland, Vance, Wake, and Warren.

THE WESTERN: Alexander, Alleghany, Anson, Ashe, Avery, Buncombe, Cabarrus, Caldwell, Catawba, Cherokee, Clay, Cleveland, Davidson, Davie, Forsyth, Gaston, Graham, Haywood, Henderson, Iredell, Jackson, Lincoln, McDowell, Macon, Madison, Mecklenburg, Mitchell, Montgomery, Polk, Rowan, Rutherford, Stanly, Stokes, Surry, Swain, Transylvania, Union, Watauga, Wilkes, Yadkin, and Yancey.[13]

First Meeting

The Southeastern District was the first to get organized, holding its convention November 7, 1936 at Fayetteville State Normal. Approximately nine hundred were in attendance and fees in the amount of $597 were collected. H. V. Brown was elected President. In the words of Dr. Charlotte Hawkins Brown, "The District Plan is already a success."

12. N. C. Teachers Record, January 1935, p. 7.

13. N. C. Teachers Record, October 1936, p. 62.

The second meeting was the Northeastern, organized at Elizabeth City on November 14, 1936. Approximately four hundred were in attendance and $274 in fees were collected. S. D. Williams was elected President.

The third meeting, the Piedmont, was held at A. & T. College December 5, 1936. Approximately nine hundred teachers were in attendance and fees to the amount of $531 were collected. J. A. Tarpley was elected President.

The final meeting, the Western District, was held in Asheville December 11, 1936, at the Stephens-Lee High School. Approximately three hundred were in attendance and $251 in fees collected. J. H. Michael was elected President.[14]

With a possible exception of the Piedmont, all the districts were too large for a one day's meeting and to permit all to return home without travel inconvenience. The Southeastern in 1951, solved this problem by agreeably dividing into two districts, the Coastal Plains and the Southeastern. In 1959 the Western divided into the Western District and the Southwestern District and by the fall of 1960, the Northeastern and the Piedmont will complete the District expansion as follows: Northeastern District and North Central District out of the old Northeastern and the Piedmont and East Piedmont out of the old Piedmont, thus increasing the total number to eight districts.[15]

Delegate Assembly

It will be recalled that the original plan for the organization of districts contained a plan for voting by delegates at the business meetings and for state officers in the local units. However, this proposal failed repeatedly to get convention approval. The districts had been organized in 1936, but it was not until 1949, thirteen years later that the delegate assembly was finally adopted. Oddly enough at that time H. V. Brown was President of the Association and also oddly was it that the convention was meeting at this time in Charlotte where the district plan had been adopted in 1936.[16]

The first delegate assembly in the history of the Association met in the 1950 convention in Raleigh. The membership at that time had risen to 7,650 and 718 delegates registered to represent that membership at the business session.[17]

However, the voting in local units for state officers was not activated until 1951 when three members of the executive committee were elected by votes of teachers in their local units. In 1952 in the first general election held after the adoption of the Delegate Assem-

14. *Ibid.*, January 1937, p. 11.
15. *Ibid.*, May 1960, p. 3.
16. *Ibid.*, May 1949, p. 72.
17. *Ibid.*, May 1950, p. 8.

bly, all officers of the Association were elected by votes of teachers in the local units. C. L. Blake, Principal of the West Charlotte High School became the first president elected by votes of the teachers and received 3,796 votes to 2,208 votes for W. I. Morris, a total of 6,004 votes.[18] Thus the ultimate objective, complete democracy in the Association had at last been achieved.

Professional Development

The tone of this study thus far might bear implications that the North Carolina Teachers Association had been an organization void of political maneuvering as Charlotte Hawkins Brown had feared in 1922 when W. A. Robinson first proposed district associations, but that is far from what has actually been the case, especially so far as the mass of the rank and file has been concerned. Most of the class-room teachers, before real democracy was achieved, spent their time in the small group meetings where the core of professionalism existed. Selection of officers had often been made by a small coterie of the leaders, college presidents, principals and others while most of the teachers had little or no voice in the choosing of officers.

Yet the Association must be credited with presenting to the teachers some of the greatest exponents of educational philosophy to be found anywhere. It cannot be denied that their contributions had a great and salutary effect upon all who heard them and, without doubt, created a greater zeal for professional improvement back home.

In addition to these general speakers the Association provided professional groups which have developed into an expanded program which reaches teachers of every phase of educational endeavor.

The Daniels Plan

Before 1950 the sectional meetings were composed mostly of the following: Elementary section, High School section, and the College section. As the Association began to grow, other groups such as Teacher Training, Supervisors, Teachers of English, Mathematics and other courses began to sprout.

Dr. R. P. Daniels, President of Shaw University, submitted a plan by which greater coordination with relationship to Association budget and the ultimate objectivity of the groups could be obtained. This plan, called "structural organization," was adopted in Charlotte at the 1949 convention.[19]

The Structural Organization is as follows:

I Division of School Administration which includes

18. *Ibid.*, May 1952, p. 18.

19. *Ibid.*, May 1949, p. 21.

A. Department of Supervisors
B. Department of Principals
 1. Section of Elementary Principals
 2. Section of Secondary Principals
II Division of Higher Education
A. Department of Administration
B. Department of Instruction
C. Department of Future Teachers
III Division of Classroom Teachers
A. Department of Elementary Teachers
 1. Section of Primary-Kindergarten Teachers
 2. Section of Grammar Grade Teachers
B. Department of Secondary Teachers
 1. Section of English
 2. Section of Foreign Languages
 3. Section of Social Studies
 4. Section of Mathematics and Science
IV Division of Special Education
A. Department of Home Economics
B. Department of Vocational Agriculture
C. Department of Industrial Education
D. Department of Music
E. Department of Health and Physical Education
F. Department of Business Education
G. Department of Extension Education
H. Department of Librarians
I. Department of Guidance

By 1959 some additional sections had crept in and with a total Association budget of $64,347.53 for 1958-59 all divisions, departments and sections were adequately activated.[20]

More far reaching than the meetings of these groups at convention time has been the expansion of the Division of Classroom Teachers into a subsidiary of the State Association in 1951.

Organized by Mrs. Hilda H. Fountain, as first chairman, the North Carolina Teachers Association-Classroom Teachers became the first state organization of classroom teachers to become affiliated with the National Education Association.

Under its second chairman, Mrs. Pauline B. Foster, classroom teachers groups were set up in each of the N.C.T.A. districts. One of the first local classroom teacher organizations was set up by Mrs. Belle D. McCorkle of Winston-Salem.[21]

Similar classroom organizations have since been set up in local units of many cities and counties, thus spreading educational democracy into every nook and corner of the state. The expansion

---

20. *Ibid.*, October 1959, Auditor's report.

21. *Ibid.*, p. 7.

brought two additional paid workers, W. I. Morris, first Public Relations Director, and Mrs. Edna C. Richards, first Executive Classroom Teacher secretary.

The Local Unit

Local units of teachers in some of the cities and counties existed to some degree long before the expansion program of the North Carolina Teachers Association began. By 1951 local units had been organized in practically every administrative unit in the state. The Local Unit became the basis of the democratic practice in the Association.

All fees are collected by the local units and the Delegated Assembly is made up of representatives of the local units in a ratio of 1 to 10 or major fraction thereof. Local units have their own constitutions, conduct their own professional meetings, and send delegates to the National Education Association.

Association Headquarters

For most of the years of the Association's history, there was no central office to carry on the Association's business nor to preserve its records.

When the Association began to publish the N. C. T. Record, a small office was secured on Hargett Street in Raleigh. Here, in an unattractive and incommodious room, Dr. G. E. Davis and W. L. Greene struggled to carry on the mounting business of the Association and to edit its journal. Leaders deplored the total inadequacy of this small office as not representative of the growing strength of the Association.

Membership continued to increase and with it the Association had begun to amass a reserve fund resulting from this increase in dues to $1.50. The audit for 1943-44 showed a budget of $6,000; actual expenses $5,048.88 and a balance of $951.22.[22]

At the convention of 1944, J. T. Taylor of Durham offered a motion that the Executive committee be authorized to set up a sinking fund as of 1945 of $1,000 annually designated for the purchase of a home for the North Carolina Teachers Association. The motion was adopted.[23] At the 1945 Convention, the Financial statement showed $1,000 deposited on the Building Fund.[24]

Search for a desirable site ended with purchase of the old "Lightner Building" on East Hargett Street in Raleigh October 1, 1946 for the sum of $55,000 with a down payment of $10,000.[25]

22. *Ibid.*, October 1944, p. 7.

23. *Ibid.*, May 1944, p. 10.

24. *Ibid.*, May 1945, p. 11.

25. *Ibid.*, March 1947, p. 2.

The Headquarters building was bought during the administration of James T. Taylor, President 1947-49. The mortgage was liquidated during the administration of H. V. Brown, President 1949-1951.[26]

The North Carolina Teachers Association has had a wonderful history and it would be impossible to recall or to give due credit to the names of the many who have made its history. Since 1922 the following served as president: James E. Shepard of North Carolina College; S. G. Atkins, President Winston-Salem Teachers College; W. S. Turner, Dean of Shaw University; G. E. Davis, Professor at Biddle University and long time agent for the Rosenwald fund; O. R. Pope, Principal of Booker T. Washington High School of Rocky Mount; J. H. Bias, President Elizabeth City Teachers College; Charlotte Hawkins Brown, President Palmer Memorial Institute; Rose Aggrey, Supervisor of Rowan County; J. W. Seabrook, President Fayetteville State Teachers College; H. L. Trigg, President Elizabeth City State Teachers College; James T. Taylor, Dean at North Carolina College; H. V. Brown, Principal of Dillard High School, Goldsboro; A. H. Anderson, Principal at Winston-Salem; C L. Blake, Principal West Charlotte High School; Ida H. Duncan, classroom teacher, Reidsville; S. D. Williams, President Elizabeth City State Teachers College; C. J. Barber, Principal at Garner, and W. R. Collins elected in 1960.

Many "grand old" patriots whom teachers loved, but never honored as president are personalities like C. M. Epps of Greenville; J. T. Barber of New Bern; Berry O'Kelly of Method, an educator who never attended school; L. H. Hall of Salisbury; J. H. Michael of Asheville; W. E. Chance of Parmelee and scores of others who were always on hand at every convention.

Influence of Agricultural Extension Service

A narrow connotation of education, especially to the ordinary layman, has often meant only what is learned within the walls of the school room. We know, of course, that to educate means "to draw out." Over the centuries man has been drawing out or leading out from one degree of knowledge to higher degrees of accomplishment. It has been the way of science and much of it has been outside the walls of school rooms. Yet it must be said that the schools and colleges have made a magnificent contribution in the diffusion of knowledge originated both outside and within the walls of the classroom.

Agricultural education is one of those sciences which man developed the hard way. Much of it was learned by trial and error. Such experimentation was often costly and sometimes meant years of frustration; yet all the time, the farmer was being educated even though his education was at times tainted with superstition and not science.

---

26. *Ibid.*, October 1951, pp. 5, 7—Audit of 1951.

The development of agricultural science and the subsquent establishment of the Agricultural Extension Service have been the salvation of the farmer in this country. No longer does he have to learn by "trial and error"; experimentation by government provisions has banished superstition and given the farmer a basis of work upon which he can depend.

This, in general terms, is the foundation of the Extension Service in the United States. How this program started and developed and how it has influenced the education of the Negro in North Carolina is told in the story which follows.

Federal Cooperation

While it is not the purpose of this work to chronicle the development of the agricultural organizations in other states, it is noteworthy that such movements existed in many parts of the country long before any government affiliation was thought of. Societies were formed in Philadelphia in 1785 and in Massachusetts in 1792 to acquaint their members with what was being done to improve agriculture and disseminate agricultural information. Circulars were sent out and were read by town clerks and ministers of the churches. Speakers, trained in science from such institutions as Columbia University and Rensaleer Institute were sent out to bolster the information contained in those circulars. In Ohio the Legislature of 1846 created "The Ohio State Board of Agriculture." Agriculture institutes sprang up in many states of the west and as far south as Tennessee and by 1899 institutes were reported in as many as 47 states with a total attendance of 500,000 farmers. About 1904 special institutes for Negro farmers were begun.

The State Colleges which had been created by the Federal Government from the sale of western lands about the beginning of the Civil War conducted various types of extension work. In 1904 Kenyon L. Butterfield expressed to the meeting of the Association of American Agricultural Colleges and Experiment Stations the idea of extension work from the base of the land-grant colleges.

Cooperative Demonstration

Seaman A. Knapp was the originator of the Farmers' Cooperatives. He introduced better farming methods to the South and induced many Northern farmers to settle in the South and many natives to undertake better farming methods. Congress appropriated $40,000 to Knapp as an emergency "to bring home to the farmer, on his own farm, information which would enable him to grow cotton despite the presence of the weevil."[27]

---

27. Lincoln David Kelsey and Cannon Chiles Hearne, *Cooperative Extension Work*, pp. 13, 18.

In 1914 the Federal Government took over the Farmers Cooperative Demonstration work with the passage of the famous Smith-Lever Act. A director of extension was appointed in each state, and B. W. Kilgore, state chemist in the Department of Agriculture, became first director in North Carolina; C. R. Hudson, first State Farm Demonstration Agent and Jane McKimmon the first State Home Demonstration Agent.[28]

Since this study is on the education of the Negroes in North Carolina, it naturally must extol the activities of those dedicated Negro pioneers who raised the dignity of the farmers and those wonderful Negro women who inspired the farm wives to a greater appreciation of rural living. They not only taught farmers and farm wives that they could advance their economic status on the farm, but they gave farm boys and girls a new appraisal of their status not as "country children" but as future citizens of the state.

Although the Smith-Lever Act was not adopted until 1914, some counties in the state were employing Negro farm demonstrators with the cooperation of farmers themselves. Among the pioneers were C. S. Mitchell of Gates County, Oliver Carter of Parmelee, G. W. Herring of Sampson, and L. E. Hall of Columbus County.

Hall, familiarly known as "Captain Hall," now living in Florida and in his eighties, writes:

> When I began as Negro Farm Demonstration Agent, Negro agents were appointed when Negroes of a county pledged $1,000 per year. Miss Emma McDougal spent her summer vacation and some of her money during the summer of 1912 getting the Negroes of Columbus County to pledge ten dollars each to raise $1,000. Upon this assumption, C. R. Hudson appointed me agent of Columbus County. Needless to say this pledge was never paid, except partially in eggs, meat, meal, syrup—anything that a fellow could chew, no matter about digestion.[29]

Captain Hall later became a District Agent covering several eastern counties of the state. Although there have been many able farm and district agents, the role of Hall is so unique that it bears special notice here.

From the Greensboro Daily News of December 15, 1922 comes this story copied verbatim:

> Masked Men Near Chadbourn, Whip Negro Extension Agent—L. E. Hall, Negro with Good Reputation Tells How. Sometime between mid-night of December 6 and one o'clock of December 7 a citizen of Columbus County was aroused at his home in Chadbourn and upon appearing at the door was confronted by a group of men wearing masks

---

28. Jane S. McKimmon, *When We're Green, We Grow*, p. v., Introduction.

29. L. E. Hall, Personal letter, December, 1958.

and robes, one of whom demanded that the householder come into the yard. Several guns were pointed in his direction. He complied, and then asked, "Now here I am, what do you want?"

"We will tell you when we take you down the road a piece," a voice replied.

"Don't take him without his clothes," someone said.

One of the masks went into the house and brought out the clothes. The householder, partially dressed, and with guns still trained on him, entered one of the several automobiles, standing in front of his place as directed.

The man who was prisoner is L. E. Hall, Negro, teacher, expert farmer, in the employ of the State of North Carolina and the United States. He is an agent in the cooperative extension work in agriculture and home economics. The head of the department is Dr. B. W. Kilgore, director of the agricultural extension service. Hall is the appointee of C. R. Hudson, state agent. These field agents receive their pay in part from the state treasury and in part from the national treasury.

At a bend in the road leading out of Chadbourn, one of the men in the car with Hall suggested that he look back, and in doing so he counted the headlights of seven automobiles. (A flour sack had been placed over the head of the prisoner; the lights were visible through it.) The captive was told there were three more cars ahead. Something was said about a whipping. It was evident there must be about 40 men in the mob.

"Good land!" said the prisoner, "does it take all those men to whip one man?" "No," he was told, "we have brought along some for witnesses."

After about three minutes the procession stopped, and a whispered conversation among the masks took place. The prisoner was told that he would be asked some questions before further procedure. The ensuing colloquy was something like this, according to Hall:

Q: Did you say that the Dyer Anti-Lynching bill would pass, and that for every Negro lynched the white people would have to pay $18,000?

A: No, I did not say that.

Q: Well, did you say that if the Dyer Anti-lynching bill did not pass, that the Negroes would stop lynching by lynching a few white people?

A: No, I never gave utterance to any such statement.

Q: What do you do around Chadbourn?

A: I don't do much of anything around Chadbourn.

Q: What kind of work do you do?

A: Extension work.

Q: Who employs you?

A: I am employed by the extension service, department of agriculture.

Q: What do you do?

A: Organize and work with Negro farmers throughout the state.

Q: That is just what we understand. You are organizing Negroes against whites throughout the state.

A: That is not so. My business is to assist farmers to do better farming and help them solve their farm problems.

Q: We did not come here to hear an agricultural lecture. Take him boys and whip him some anyhow.

The Negro was directed to sit down on a ditch bank and spreading his coat on the ground he did so. After which one of the masks beat him for a while.

"Haven't you anything to say?" Hall was asked. "No, I have nothing to say," was the reply. Another period of beating with what appeared to be a wet rope, but it may have been a strap.

"Now stop and let him talk," said the monitor. The prisoner said that if they would tell him what they wanted him to say he would try to say it. "We know what you are doing, but we want to hear you say it." As a rejoinder, "I am not doing anything I have not told you," said Hall.

They beat him some more, turned his face toward home and told him if he would go in the direction he was headed he would land there. He told them he thought the sack might come off his head and they agreed. He was able to recognize no one in the party and to see none of the cars bore license tags. The beating was severe but left no permanent injury.

The Greensboro Daily News went on to write:

Hall is black, something between six feet and six two in stature, powerfully built. He is an upstanding man and carries himself with an air of unquestionably belonging on the earth. He says he has never harmed anybody in his life, has a conscience void of offense, and made up his mind from the first to take whatever was given him without resistance, as resistance of 40 by one—the forty having arms, too would be foolish. He relates his experience calmly and says he talked with the mob in ordinary conversational tone.

The Daily News continues:

There is a great variety of types among Negroes of full blood, a transmission of the variety of tribal types from which they sprang. To this day some African Tribes are pacific, some warlike; some proud, intelligent, bold; some mean and timorous. Hall conveys the impression that fear

127

of man is foreign to his nature. He insists he was not frightened on this occasion, and his manner in saying it carries conviction. He is an educated man, accustomed to address crowds, and he expresses himself with simple, concise dignity and eloquence. He is not very widely known in the Chadbourn neighborhood, being absent most of the time among farmers.

Hall has been a co-worker with Frissell, Booker Washington and Dr. Moton and has been thoroughly imbued with the Booker Washington doctrine as to the place and duty of Negro Citizenship—let politics alone, be clean, strive toward intelligence, be industrious, leave the social and political structure entirely in the hands of the white man. His identity with the group, the fact that he has been an employee of the state under the immediate supervision of Mr. Hudson, who appointed him for eight years, and that the activities of these farm agents are open records, seem to preclude the possibility of Hall's being a raciopolitical propagandist.

Hall says, it is bad enough to be beaten, but the experience has left a question in his mind that is more serious. Washington preached, Moton exhorts, Newbold proclaims that intelligence and industry and frugality will solve the race problem.

"For 15 years since graduating from Hampton, there has not been a work day that I did not get pay for. Many nights and sometimes Sundays I have worked. I own the house in which I live and eight lots adjoining it. My house is painted and has six rooms. I have a small farm. I have endeavored to mind my own business and meddle with no man's private life. If this is not the type of citizenship required of us, then what is required? If a man who tends to his own business is not safe with his family in a home that he has bought and paid for, then where can he be safe?

"These reflections are far sadder than the beating itself, because they seem to present a hopeless situation."
The Daily News concludes:

District Agent Hall's name is found in "Who's Who in Agriculture" published by L. H. Bailey of Cornell University. He was a member of the inter-racial committee appointed by Governor Bickett during the World War, and is a member of the executive committee of the Negro Farmers Conference of North Carolina.[30]

R. E. Jones, Negro State Agent and Mrs. Minnie M. Brown, Assistant State Negro Home Demonstration Agent, give the following summary of Agricultural Extension Service and its influence upon the education of the Negro.

---

30. Greensboro Daily News, December 15, 1922.

R. E. JONES
Assistant State Agent
Agricultural Extension Service

MINNIE MILLER BROWN
State Home Agent

129

The early objectives of the Extension Service were: (1) to increase the net income of farmers through efficient production and marketing and the better use of capital and credit; (2) to promote better homes and a higher standard of living on farms; (3) to develop rural leaders; (4) to promote the mental, social, cultural, recreational, and community life of rural people; (5) to implant a love for rural life among farm boys and girls; (6) to acquaint the public with the place of agriculture in our national life; (7) to enlarge the vision of rural people and the nation on rural matters; and (8) to improve the educational and spiritual life of rural people.

The first Negro county agent was Neal Alexander Bailey, who began work November 1, 1910. He was a native of Chatham County and was graduated from A. and T. College at the age of fifty years. He served Guilford, Randolph, and Rockingham counties. Among the early agents (Hall, Carter, and C. S. Mitchell already mentioned) were W. D. Brown, of Hertford; S. T. Brooks, of Robeson, J. D. Carver, of Rowan, D. D. Dupree, of Green, J. W. Mitchell, of Columbus and Bladen, and L. R. Sanders, of Johnston.

Some of the first Home Demonstration agents were Emma McDougald, of Wayne, Margaurite Galloway, of Wake, Lucy Wade, of Johnston, Carrie Spaulding, of Columbus, Sarah Williams, of Beaufort, and Cherry Fulton, of Anson.

The main objectives of Extension Service, after a half century of expansion and development are as follows: (1) Efficiency in agricultural production; (2) marketing, distribution, and utilization of farm products; (3) conservation and wise use of and development of natural resources; (4) management on the farm and in the home; (5) family living; (6) youth development; (7) leadership development; (8) community improvement and resource development; and (9) public affairs.

Organizations and expansion emerging from Extension Service include the following:

The 4-H Club Foundation of North Carolina, Incorporated
The State Council of Home Demonstration Clubs
The Western District
The Northeastern District and
Southeastern District Home Demonstration Councils
The State Conference of Farmers and Homemakers
Town and Rural Life Ministers Institute
State 4-H Club Recognition Program
Southeastern District
Northeastern District and
Western District Recognition Programs
4-H Club camp at Hammocks Beach, built in 1955 at a cost of $125,000.

The Agricultural Extension Service is an out of school educational system represented by three levels of government—Federal, State, and County. It is charged with the responsibility of providing information of an educational nature in agriculture and home economics and related areas to non-residents of State College and with the thought that they are to encourage the adoption of the program, predicated on a utility aspect for the citizens of the State.

North Carolina has gone from approximately three county agents in 1910 to a total of 137 county agricultural and home economic extension agents, 16 state staffed people and 54 clerical workers, making a total of 120 employed persons in the State with the organization.

The present staff (1960) consists of State Agent, R. E. Jones, Assistant State Home Demonstration Agent, Minnie Miller Brown, District Agricultural Agents, J. A. Spaulding, L. R. Johnson and H. M. McNeill; District Home Economics Agents: Wilhelmina R. Laws, F. W. Corbett, and J. S. Weaver; Home Economics Subject Matter Specialists: B. B. Ramseur and G. K. Greenlee; Technical Agricultural Specialists: R. L. Wynn, S. J. Hodges, T. W. Flowers, P. P. Thompson; and 4-H Club leaders: W. C. Cooper and Helen Branford.[31]

The story of the Extension Service began with a unique "Captain Hall," and ends with another unique character, "Ham Johnson."

This unique personality, L. R. Johnson, long time county agent in Johnston County now a District agent, had long conducted "ham shows" to encourage better production of country cured hams. He became popularly known as "Ham Johnson."

Editor Henry Belk, of the Goldsboro News Argus, August 29, 1960, comments as follows:

A few years from now you will be able to find more country hams and of superior quality.

Negro farmers are doing their part in this direction. Credit the Johnston County Ham Show experiment started years ago with great influence in servicing man with that joyous delight, real country ham. Negro Farm Agent, L. R. Johnson made the Johnston show at Smithfield one which reached hundreds of farmers and became a show known beyond the bounds of the state.

Transferred a couple of years ago to Greensboro as Western District agricultural agent for the Extension Service, Johnson the past year took the ham show idea to 13 Piedmont counties. Negro farmers exhibited hundreds of hams at the shows. First object in the shows is to improve quality. So only about eight of the shows also conducted sales. The idea will be extended for the coming years with the public given a chance to bid for quality country-cured meats.[32]

31. R. E. Jones, Negro State Agent; Minnie Miller Brown, Assistant State Negro Home Demonstration Agent, Official Data, Agricultural Extension Service.

32. Goldsboro News-Argus, Editorial, August 29, 1960.

L. E. HALL
*Pioneer Farm Demonstration Agent
Agricultural Extension Service*

L. R. JOHNSON
District Agent, Agricultural Extension Service

132

Like "Captain" Hall, L. R. (Ham) Johnson was elevated to a District agent and like the many other dedicated men and women of the Extension Service went far beyond the ordinary duties and responsibilities of his own county in influencing education through the medium of the ham show.

Education of Nurses

About the turn of the century, a Negro nurse was scarcely more than what we term today, a "baby sitter"; functioning only in the custodial care of children of the well-to-do. To be sure many Negro women had been nurses to elders, particularly the aged, but they were almost wholly without scientific training.

Saint Agnes Hospital

According to Cecil Halliburton, a professor at Saint Augustine's College,[33] the first efforts toward training of nurses began with the establishment of Saint Agnes Hospital on the campus of Saint Augustine's College in Raleigh in 1896.

In 1895, Mrs. A. B. Hunter, wife of the principal of Saint Augustine's, attended a missionary convention in Minneapolis. She made a stirring appeal for funds to set up a much needed hospital at that institution. A Mr. I. L. Collins from California gave the first money, $600, and an anonymous donor $500 toward the erection of the hospital. The institution was named "Saint Agnes" in memory of the wife of Mr. Collins whose first name was Agnes. The building was dedicated October 18, 1896 and thus became the first nurse training school for Negroes in the State of North Carolina.

Mrs. A. B. Hunter served as superintendent and the first head nurse was Miss Marie L. Burgess. The first class started numbered four students and one of the first to graduate was a Miss Claudia West Brown of Goldsboro now living in Norwich, Connecticut.

A modern stone building was erected in 1928-29 when the institution was accredited by the State. The largest class was graduated in 1956 with fifteen members.

The institution discontinued the training of nurses in 1959 as the erection of a county hospital contemplated the assumption of nursing education in the area.[34]

Lincoln Hospital, Durham

Lincoln Hospital, Durham, was founded in 1901 by Dr. A. M. Moore, Durham's first Negro physician; Dr. S. L. Warren, and John Merrick. The occasion of its founding was a desire on the part of Washington Duke to show his appreciation for the service Negroes

33. Cecil Haliburton, *History of Saint Augustine's College*, 1937, pp. 21, 22.

34. Interview, Georgia Alston Jones, Director of Nurses, St. Agnes Hospital, Raleigh, North Carolina.

had rendered toward the South in the dark days of the Civil War. He proposed a monument on the campus of Trinity College (now Duke University).

He was convinced by Moore, Warren, and Merrick that a hospital was much more needed and would be much more useful to the descendants of slaves than a marble slab on the campus of Trinity College where Negroes did not even attend.

Duke donated $8,500 and the first frame building accommodating 50 patients was built. In a few years, the demand for beds outgrew this capacity and the sons of Duke, J. B. and B. N. Duke, agreed to donate $75,000 provided the trustees could raise a similar amount. The city of Durham and Durham County each donated $25,000 and the citizens raised $25,000 making the total of $75,-000.

The present brick structure was thus assured and erected in 1929. It has been improved and in 1952 an enlargement, bringing the bed capacity to 125 and bassinets for babies to 25 was added.

The institution began training nurses in 1903. The requirements at that time were rather low and consisted of only two years. The course now is three years and provides affiliated training in Pediatrics at Meharry Medical School in Nashville, Tennessee, and also in Psychiatry at Crownsville State Hospital in Maryland. Students spend the first nine months in concentrated study in all sciences at North Carolina College.

Students come from many parts of the United States.

We are happy to say that some of the best students have come to us from Dillard High School in Goldsboro.

The institution has graduated more than 500 nurses since its organization and they are serving throughout the United States and abroad. Among them, Mrs. Della Rainey Robinson was the first Negro nurse to be made a captain in the United States Army in World War II, and reached the rank of Major. Miss Mary Mills is with U. S. Public Health Service and has served 12 years in Liberia and Lebanon under the Government's Point Four Program. She organized a school of nursing in Liberia.

Miss Mills received the M. S. degree in Public Health Nursing at New York University and has done further study at Johns Hopkins University. She studied political science at Bierut College for Women in Lebanon and has been honored with decorations by both Liberia and Lebanon. She holds an honorary degree from Tuskegee Institute.[35]

Community Hospital, Wilmington

This institution, which has had a very fine record in the training of nurses, was established by a group of progressive Negro citizens

---

35. William M. Rich, Director, Lincoln Hospital, Durham, N. C., Special report.

of Wilmington in 1920. Among them were The Reverend W. H. Moore, The Reverend A. J. Wilson, Dr. John W. Kay, and Dr. Foster Burnett. Under their leadership, Negro citizens raised the first funds for the purchase of a frame building at 717 North Seventh Street. The building was equipped as well as it could be with the limited amount of money at the disposal of the Negro citizens.

In 1923, The Honorable Emmett Bellamy, New Hanover County's representative in the State Legislature, was instrumental in securing an act passed by the Legislature empowering the New Hanover County Commissioners to take over and to operate the hospital. In 1930, under a joint cooperative effort of the County Commissioners and the City Commission of Wilmington, funds were secured from the Federal Government for the erection of a modern building on land donated by the Board of Education of New Hanover County. The facilities were expanded to a capacity of 104 beds.

The first medical staff consisted of five Negro physicians, Doctors H. A. Coddington, Foster Burnett, Ernest Bullock, Houston Moore, and Frank Avant. The first superintendent of nurses was Miss Salomie Taylor. The medical staff also included two white doctors and has remained interracial in composition.

The Ladies Auxiliary, an organization founded by Mrs. Irene Maides in 1922, has been of great help to the hospital in providing free service, linen, decorations, and other needs provided in its budget.

The first administrator of Community Hospital was Frank Adair, who had been an administrative assistant at Sydenham Hospital in New York City. The present Hospital Board (1960) consists of the following: Colonel A. P. Kelley, retired U. S. Army physician, chairman; E. M. Butler, vice chairman; T. V. Love, county auditor; Peter Braak, county commissioner; B. P. Adkins, W. D. Campbell, W. M. Cameron, Dr. H. A. Eaton, and A. E. Gibson.

Community Hospital has had a long record of training nurses and is continuing that function when most of the hospitals are abandoning it.[36]

Those that have been closed are L. Richardson in Greensboro, Good Samaritan in Charlotte and St. Agnes in Raleigh.

Kate Bittings-Reynolds maintains an affiliation with Winston-Salem Teachers College and L. Richardson with A. and T. College. All have made a commendable contribution in the field of Nurse Education.

Some county hospitals have made some effort toward training practical nurses. Wayne County Hospital in 1957 trained a number of practical nurses most of whom have been employed in Wayne County at Cherry Hospital and the O'Berry School.

---

36. E. M. Butler, Vice Chairman, Community Hospital, Wilmington, N. C. Special report.

That the strong must bear the infirmities of the weak has been well recognized by the state. So long as any delinquency or deprivation exists, the State feels a sense of responsibility, and stands ready to act.

The General Assembly of 1917 enacted the legislation which is the foundation of the county-administered State-supervised program of public welfare in North Carolina. The services and financial grants have come more and more to be understood as a strengthening factor in the economy of the state. More public understanding of the underlying causes of social problems has brought with it increased understanding of public welfare's role in modern society.[37]

Through N. C. Newbold, a grant from the Laura Spellman-Rockefeller Memorial fund, the Negro unit of welfare work was set up in 1925. L. A. Oxley was its first consultant.

The consultant on work among Negroes of the State Department Public Welfare, attempts to work with all organizations (local, state-wide and national) to improve the social and economic conditions among Negroes in the State. There has been some affiliation of the North Carolina Federation of Negro Women's Clubs in pointing out the needs for an institution for delinquent girls. Such an institution already mentioned in Chapter VII was first set up at Efland through the efforts of the Women's Clubs and later assumed by the State; now operating at Dobb's Farm near Kinston.

Lieutenant Oxley (as he was better known) resigned in 1934 and was succeeded by the Reverend William Randolph Johnson who served until 1942 when John R. Larkins was appointed.

Larkins, well trained and endowed with discreet urbanity, has pursued the work with great respect and ability. He is author of a book, "Patterns of Negro Leadership," 1959 and is also widely sought as a commencement speaker.

In an interview with Larkins, he pointed out:

It is somewhat difficult to point out what I consider the most important contribution this area of work has made to Negro education. It is my belief that through the making of scientific studies in the social and economic conditions among Negroes in the State, it has been possible to create an awareness of some of the areas of unmet needs. After this information was secured, the consultant would meet with various fraternal, civic, and religious groups to discuss these needs. Conferences were held with the Governors, State Legislators, and other influential white and

---

37. Biennial Report, North Carolina State Board of Public Welfare, July 1956, June 1, 1958, p. 9.

JOHN R. LARKINS
State Consultant, Negro Welfare

Negro citizens to acquaint them with these conditions. In my estimation, this has been an area in which important contributions have been made.[38]

Summary

The class room and the college have been greatly bolstered in their activities by the contingent influences mentiond in this chapter which have contributed immeasurably to the education of Negroes in North Carolina.

For more than three quarters of a century the North Carolina Teachers Association has fostered the growth of professionalism which inspired and cultivated higher standards of teaching and consequently more profound sense of learning among children. Its growth and expansion have been so phenomenal that very few public school teachers remain outside the pale of its influence. Opportunities for leadership and individual participation are now prime functions of local units in every part of the state.

The Agricultural Extension Service has tapped the grass roots of educational growth in that it associates itself with the basic needs of human existence; food, clothing, and shelter. The promotion and development of the 4-H Program (Head, Heart, Hand, and Health) has had a tremendous effect upon the evaluation and appreciation of rural life among boys and girls. Perhaps the greatest contribution made by the Extension Service to the education of the youth is that it has demonstrated immediate use of education through the 4-H Program as well as to heighten the standard of citizenship among its members.

Nurse education had a delayed beginning in the education of Negroes and, despite the fact that the early nurse training hospitals are discontinuing the training, nurse education is taking on a new emphasis as several colleges are including it in their curriculum. The prospect for much needed practical nursing programs is also gaining strength with the erection of adequate county hospitals in many parts of the state.

Public Welfare functions have made the citizenship of the state keenly aware of its duties and responsibilities to the handicapped and the delinquent. The public is no longer so complacent as to close its eyes to conditions which can be easily corrected or which might not have existed if there had been recognition and acceptance of the philosophy, "The Strong must bear the infirmities of the Weak."

---

38. J. R. Larkin, Negro Consultant, State Department of Public Welfare, Interview.

Chapter IX

Influence Of Negroes In The State Department Of Education

Much has been said in Chapter V as to the role of N. C. Newbold who spearheaded the greatest period of educational activity among Negroes for more than thirty years. To him must go the credit for the establishment of the Negro Division of Education as an auxiliary of the State Department of Public Instruction. Without this set-up there might not have been the remarkable concentration of effort which has resulted in the incredible era of progress among schools of the state.

The Negro Division was established by Legislative Act in 1921 and Newbold was its first Director. He had an able assistant in G. H. Ferguson who succeeded him upon retirement. Aside from his Assistant Director, Newbold secured two dynamic Negro agents whose contributions were widely heralded all over the state. They were Annie W. Holland, Supervisor of Elementary Education and W. A. Robinson, High School Inspector.

Mrs. Holland is depicted in Newbold's book, "Five Negro Educators," mentioned earlier in this story. She had long been identified with the organization of rural clubs as means toward improving education. She had also served as State Home Demonstration Agent in 1915.[1]

In 1923-24 Mrs. Holland started a movement to organize local parent-teacher associations. Many community leagues changed into parent-teacher associations, and soon county-wide organizations were formed. Out of these local and county parent-teacher associations the North Carolina Congress of Parents and Teachers was organized in 1927, holding its first annual meeting at Shaw University on April 14, 1928. The number of associations at this first annual meeting was 784 and the membership was 15,770. The amount of money raised during the year was over $50,000.

Mrs. Holland proved her ability as a teacher in the classroom and community worker in the school, church, and home. As State Supervisor she labored earnestly toward the improvement of elementary schools. Her greatest contribution undoubtedly was the founding and promotion of the North Carolina Congress of Colored Parents and Teachers.[2]

Like Aycock, who died addressing an educational meeting in Birmingham, she died in 1934 addressing an educational meeting at Louisburg in Franklin County.[3]

---

1. Newbold, N. C., *Five Negro Educators*, p. 77.

2. *Ibid.*, p. 81.

3. North Carolina Teachers Record, January 1934, p. 5.

MRS. ANNIE W. HOLLAND, *State Supervisor*
First Appointed by Newbold, 1915

W. A. ROBINSON

H. L. TRIGG

W. A. Robinson, a stepson of the incomparable James E. Shepard, had been a successful high school teacher in Louisville, Kentucky. As High School Inspector, Robinson was committed to a program of standardization in line with standards of the Southern Association of Secondary Schools and Colleges.

During his tenure, 1921-28, forty-two high schools were accredited by the state as 4-year standard high schools and 19 of these were approved by the Southern Association of Secondary Schools and Colleges.[4]

Robinson not only served as High School Inspector, but was also Corresponding Secretary of the North Carolina Teachers Association. In addition, as aid to Newbold, he helped set up the system of county summer schools to aid those teachers who were unable to attend the larger summer schools.

H. L. Trigg, who later headed two colleges in the state, succeeded Robinson and served as High School Inspector from 1928 to 1939. Trigg had previously served as Principal of the Berry O'Kelly Training School at Method and at Atkins High School of Winston-Salem. He was the son of an early President of Bennett College, Dr. Frank Trigg, and was educated at Morgan College, Baltimore.

Well trained in the duties of supervision, Trigg continued the program of standardization which had been started by Robinson. During the time he served, he saw the colleges discontinue secondary work and enter upon a program of exclusive college training thus causing the most revolutionary activity among local boards of education the State had ever known. Grammar schools developed into high schools and high schools not only added on extra years, but increased in efficiency. High School graduates in 1929 had numbered only 1,687. By 1940 the number had increased to 4,839.

While Trigg was on a leave of absence in 1937, Nelson H. Harris, professor of education at Shaw University, filled the position as supervisor. Trigg resigned in 1939 to become President of Elizabeth City State Teachers College.

Albert E. Manley

Graduating "cum laude" from Johnson C. Smith University in 1930, Manley successively held positions as high school teacher and as the principal of Stephens-Lee High School in Asheville. He earned the Master's degree from Columbia University and the Doctor's degree from Stanford University. Following a leave of absence in 1943, during which time J. B. McRae, Dean of Fayetteville State Teachers College and S. E. Duncan, principal of Washington High School at Reidsville, filled the gap, Manley resigned the position to become Dean of the College of Arts and Science at North Carolina College in Durham. He later became president of Spellman College in Atlanta.[5]

4. Report, Office of the Director—Negro Division of Education, February 14, 1958.

5. Profile, A. E. Manley, State High School Supervisor.

Samuel E. Duncan

Born in Salisbury, North Carolina, Duncan received his college education at Livingstone College where he was graduated in 1927. He earned the M. A. degree at Cornell University in 1932 and the Ph. D. degree at Cornell University in 1949. Aside from holding positions as a high school teacher and as a principal, he has had a wide range of educational experiences in college summer schools in several states. For twelve years he served as state high school supervisor in North Carolina and was a potent force for good relationships between the Department of Public Instruction and local administrative units with regard to the development of Negro high schools in the state.

From Duncan's own memoranda of his philosophy and practices, a clear picture of the basis for his long standing success as a high school supervisor can be seen. Some of these guiding principles follow.

1. Evaluation of our task would be more valid perhaps if done by those whom we serve, the staff members with whom we labor, and those who supervise our work.

2. Evaluation is a continuous process with few movements or projects being completed in the absolute.

3. The role of the Negro State Supervisor is undergoing a gradual change; some of the factors involved being:

   a. The employment of a larger number of instructional supervisors in local administrative units

   b. The changing complex of public education

   c. The clearer distinction between supervision and administration

   d. The organizational changes in functions of various divisions in the State Department of Education, and

   e. The impact of the Supreme Court Decision related to segregation in public schools.

4. State supervision, as administered by members of the Division of Negro Education, is general and comprehensive; thus it embraces many aspects of the educational program and at times approaches the boundary line of administration.

In approaching our duties, we attempt to keep in mind that:

1. The regulations, policies, and interests of the State Department of Education should remain prominent in the execution of all assignments.

2. Unity of purpose and harmonious relations should be evident on the part of the personnel of the Division and the Department.

3. The ultimate authority for the improvement of instruction and the employment and releasing of personnel to effect such, rests with the local administrative unit.

4. We endeavor to be tactful and to remember that friendliness begets friendliness. However, the pointing out of errors, deficiencies, and making suggestions for improvement should be done as necessarily as identifying those features that are commendable in a situation.[6]

Duncan resigned the position as State Supervisor of Negro high schools in 1958 when he was elected president of Livingstone College in Salisbury.

Frank A. Tolliver

A survey of the quality of educators who have served with the State Department indicates that the state affords many able personalities ready to step in as others are elevated to larger spheres of usefulness. Such indeed is the case of a successor to Duncan.

Educated at Atlanta University where he earned his Bachelor's degree; at the University of Michigan for the degree of Master of Arts; and at Columbia University where he earned the degree of Doctor of Education, Frank A. Tolliver was eminently fitted to assume the appointment as state supervisor of Negro high schools. His educational experience as a high school teacher, as a principal at Statesville, as principal of the Stephens-Lee High School in Asheville, and as an instructor at Tennessee A. and I. University augmented his professional training in three of the nation's best universities.[7]

With so rich a background of training and experience, Dr. Tolliver brought to the State Department a great potentiality which would reflect itself in a continuation of the great work of his predecessors.

Women In the State Department

Following the death of Mrs. Annie W. Holland, Pearl Smothers-Byrd (now Mrs. Pearl Larsen) became the Negro State Supervisor of Elementary Schools. Mrs. Larsen was graduated from Hampton Institute and for several years was the Jeanes Supervisor in Wake County. Dr. Newbold regarded her as an able educator and, upon request of educators in the Virgin Islands, granted a leave of absence to Mrs. Larsen to conduct teachers' institutes in the islands. There she met and married a Mr. Larsen and resigned her position in North Carolina.

Marie McIver

At the unanimous request of the Jeanes supervisors, Marie McIver was appointed State Supervisor of Negro Elementary Schools succeeding Mrs. Larsen.

---

6. Memoranda, S. E. Duncan, State High School Supervisor.

7. Profile, Frank A. Tolliver, State Supervisor Negro High Schools.

144

Born in the State of Georgia, Miss McIver was educated at Saint Augustine's College in Raleigh and at Hampton Institute. She earned the M. A. degree at Columbia University. As Jeanes Supervisor in Halifax County, she held the distinction of sponsoring the building of more Rosenwald schools in that county than had been built in any other county in the entire South. All over her territory she championed the needs of Negro boys and girls as being the same as those of all other children.[8]

Following her death at Weldon, May 7, 1948, the North Carolina Teachers Record editorialized:

Miss Marie McIver, who stood in the forefront of an outstanding group of Jeanes teachers in North Carolina for over two decades, passed to her reward during the summer vacation. It may be some time before the educational forces of the state can come fully to realize her worth as a standard bearer. Miss McIver was a keen student of the educational standards for elementary schools. She sought to have these standards applied equally in every school district of the state. Her achievements, while not great in volume were outstanding in quality and character. Time will deepen our sense of appreciation for the manner in which she held aloft the banner of high standards as a goal for the teachers of our elementary schools.[9]

Minnie Ruth Lawrence-Woodson

After the retirement of Dr. Newbold, the need for and the influence of the Negro Division of Education seemed to decline, although Newbold's successor, G. H. Ferguson, never relaxed in his zeal to maintain the high quality of leadership which had been maintained by Newbold. Mr. Ferguson retired in 1960, but prior to his retirement, the supervisory program had been expanded to include three elementary supervisors. The Negro Division was merged into other services of the State Department of Public Instruction; the Negro supervisors being continued in their functions as high school and elementary supervisors. Mrs. Woodson, a native of Rocky Mount and successor to Miss McIver, became the fourth state elementary supervisor and the first native North Carolinian to hold the position. Her early training was received in the public schools of Rocky Mount, her undergraduate training at Hampton Institute, and her Master's degree from Columbia University. She has done further work in several other universities including Columbia University, University of Michigan, and Temple University. Her teaching experience has been rich and varied; first, as a classroom teacher in Rocky Mount; then as supervisor of Sampson County Negro schools; instructor in summer school at North Carolina College; and currently, State Supervisor of Negro Elementary Schools.

---

8. North Carolina Teachers Record, Article, Willie Jeffries, October 1948.

9. Editorial, North Carolina Teachers Record, October 1948.

MINNIE LAWRENCE WOODSON

DAISY WALKER ROBSON

ANNA M. COOKE

Aside from these experiences, Mrs. Woodson has been a member of the State Committee on the Improvement of Elementary Education; a member of the Board of Managers of the North Carolina Congress of Parents and Teachers; and a member of the Executive Committee of the National Hampton Alumni Association.[10]

Daisy Walker Robson

Mrs. Daisy Walker Robson had been a classroom teacher at the Richard B. Harrison High School in Selma and supervisor of the Burlington Elementary schools before being appointed to a state position in the expanded program of supervision. She earned the B. S. and the M. A. degrees at Hampton Institute and pursued further study at Northwestern and Syracuse Universities.[11]

Anna M. Cooke

Miss Anna M. Cooke received her early education in Harrisburg, Pennsylvania. Her undergraduate work was done at Wilberforce University and at Winston-Salem Teachers College. She earned the Master of Education degree at Pennsylvania State University where she is currently (1960) a candidate for a degree of Doctor of Education.

Miss Cooke has had extensive experience in nursery school education; as a classroom teacher; as an associate professor of elementary education and supervising teacher at a laboratory school at Wilberforce University; and as a county supervisor of schools in North Carolina. Currently (1960)[12] she is one of the state supervisors of elementary schools.

While these state workers were originally responsible directly to the Negro Division of Education under Newbold and Ferguson, they were associated with other State Department workers who were attached to state institutions for the supervision of vocational agriculture, vocational trades and industries and vocational home economics.

Vocational education in the high schools emanates from the Smith-Hughes Act of 1917 which provides Federal cooperation with the states in the teaching of agriculture, industries, and home economics.

Robert E. Malone

The first Negro supervisor of vocational agriculture was Robert E. Malone who, as assistant to Roy Thomas, of State College in Raleigh, set up the first Smith-Hughes vocational agricultural pro-

10. Profile, Minnie Ruth Woodson, State Supervisor Elementary Negro Schools.

11. Profile, Daisy Walker Robson, State Supervisor Elementary Negro Schools.

12. Profile, Anna M. Cooke, State Supervisor Elementary Negro Schools.

gram among Negro high schools of the state. Malone, a native of the State of Kentucky, was a graduate of Hampton Institute and served as supervisor until 1920 when he resigned to head an agricultural school in Arkansas.

S. B. Simmons

Succeeding Malone, Simmons served as supervisor of vocational agriculture for Negro schools until his death in 1957. During his long tenure, vocational agriculture spread to the four corners of the state in the rapidly developing rural high schools. Like the 4-H program of the Agricultural Extension Service, the program inspired rural boys and girls to combine practical experience through the "home project" with classroom activities and thus accentuate the objectivity of rural education.

With the passing of Simmons, the state saw the need for expanding the supervisory functions and provided for a supervisor in the West and one for the East, both working out from A. and T. College in Greensboro.

Walter T. Johnson, Sr.

Johnson, a native of Pender County, received his early training at the Pender County Training School, Rocky Point, where he was a student under Singleton C. Anderson (see special note). Johnson's undergraduate and graduate degrees were earned at A. and T. College. He did special study in low cost housing at Wallingford, Pennsylvania, and further study in economics at Henry George School of Social Science and at Purdue University. He taught vocational agriculture at Spring Hope, N. C., and later served as farm-shop teacher trainer at A. and T. College. From 1941 to 1948 he was assistant to S. B. Simmons, State Supervisor of Vocational Agriculture, in charge of Defense, Rural War Production, and Veteran Farmer Training programs. From 1948 to 1952, he served as itinerant teacher trainer at West Virginia State College and organized the vocational agricultural program for West Virginia among Negro schools.

Johnson returned to A. and T. College as assistant supervisor of vocational agricultural education and upon the death of S. B. Simmons, in 1957, was appointed state supervisor.

Johnson is connected with many religious, civic, and fraternal organizations and with such experience as these afford, is well equipped to keep the high quality of work which Simmons so nobly pursued.[13]

J. W. Warren, Jr.

Warren, a native of Nash County, received his early education at the Spaulding High School in Spring Hope and his college training

---

13. W. L. Johnson, Assistant State Supervisor, Vocational Agriculture.

W. T. JOHNSON, SR.
District Supervisor, Vocational Agriculture
Western North Carolina

at A. and T. College. His experience included vocational agricultural teaching at Henderson Institute in Henderson, North Carolina, and at the Franklin County Training School at Louisburg, North Carolina. His present function is similar to that of Walter T. Johnson with supervision confined to the eastern part of the state. Like Johnson, Warren is connected with a number of religious and fraternal organizations. He is a lay minister of the Seventh Day Adventist Church and serves on the executive committee of the South Atlantic Conference of his church which embraces North and South Carolina, Georgia, and Florida.[14]

Note on Vocational Agriculture

It might be remiss to tell the story of vocational agriculture in North Carolina without mentioning one of the most celebrated teachers of the subject in this state, Singleton C. Anderson, one of the pioneers of the program.

Anderson, a graduate of Hampton Institute, served for more than forty years as vocational agricultural teacher in Pender County. He was cited by Carl Goerch, editor of The State (March 16, 1946, p. 4) as having completely renovated an entire community by inducing the citizens to build new homes and practice improved methods of agriculture. One of Anderson's greatest contributions was the training of W. T. Johnson who became a state supervisor of vocational agriculture.

There have been many other teachers of vocational agriculture in the state. The author of this book, incidentally, was among the pioneers, having set up the first vocational agricultural course at the Columbus County Training School at Whiteville in 1919. But Singleton Anderson's work was perhaps the most significant example of what vocational objectivity can do for a community.

Vocational Trades; and Home Economics

Similar to the objectivity of vocational agriculture, trade and home economics education has been implemented into the school curriculum. This approach to education has been found generally in city schools while vocational agriculture is almost exclusively a rural high school program. However, the basic philosophy of combining project work with science is quite the same.

High school boys taking vocational trades are required to construct real dwellings which are sold at public auction to the highest bidder. Girls are required to pursue practical projects in home beautification, family relationships, child development, food and clothing, and health and home nursing.

Samuel C. Smith

Vocational trade education among Negro high schools had its

---

14. Profile, J. W. Warren, East District Supervisor, Vocational Agriculture.

150

J. W. Warren, Jr.
District Supervisor, Vocational Agriculture
Eastern North Carolina

Samuel C. Smith
First State Supervisor,
Vocational Trades and
Industries

Joseph R. Taylor
Second State Supervisor,
Vocational Trades and
Industries

151

SINGLETON C. ANDERSON

Pioneer Vocational Agricultural
Instructor

Here's one of the homes in the Rocky Point section that was
built under the supervision of Professor Anderson. Note the
trim hedge and shrubbery.

beginning in 1941 with S. C. Smith as the first supervisor of Negro work

Smith was educated at A. and T. College and at the University of Michigan where he earned the Master of Science degree in 1940. He had been an instructor in brick masonry at Lincoln Academy, 1929-30 and at Dillard High School in Goldsboro from 1934 to 1941 when he resigned to become the supervisor of trade and industrial education among the Negro schools. He retained this position until 1954 when he became Dean of the Technical Institute at A. and T. College.

Smith was affiliated with numerous church, civic, and fraternal organizations and was a leading official in his church. Aside from these activities, he has a long record of professional service and has written many articles for publication. His name is found in Who's Who in Colored America, 1950 edition and in Who's Who in the South and Southwest, 1950 edition.[15]

James R. Taylor

Smith was succeeded as supervisor of Trade Education by James R. Taylor, of Mississippi who received his early education at Alcorn College in that state and his graduate training at the University of Minnesota where he earned the M. A. degree. His experience included teaching of building trades and supervision of trade and industrial education in his native state. Aside from his professional experience, Taylor had three years of military service in the United States army. Since assuming the position as supervisor, he has seen a state wide program of trade development manifested in more than a quarter million dollars' worth of building construction done by high school students.[16]

Lucy Fuller James

Born in Franklinton, North Carolina, Mrs. James was educated at Shaw University, Pratt Institute, Columbia University, and at the University of Chicago. She earned the B. S. and the M. A. degrees at Columbia University.

Her educational experience includes teaching and supervision in Georgia, Texas, Delaware, West Virginia, and in North Carolina. In 1937 she became the first assistant state supervisor of home economics education. This position she has held to this date (1960).

Mrs. James is co-author of the first publication for the teaching of child development on the college level, "Course Study in Children's Clothing," published by Edwards Brothers, Inc., Ann Arbor, Michigan. She organized the North Carolina Association of Home Economists and also the first organization for Negro girls, Future

---

15. Profile, S. C. Smith, Dean Technical Institute, A. and T. College.

16. Profile, Joseph R. Taylor, Assistant State Supervisor Trade and Industrial Education.

LUCY FULLER JAMES

Homemakers of North Carolina. Her greatest contribution, perhaps, is the establishing of the Home Eckers Trade School in Raleigh, an institution for the training of young women in the food service industries. Its first graduation was held in 1950.[17]

This ends the profile of Negro educators who work at state level in what is perhaps the most important phase of public school development in the history of Negro education in this state. At least their role has been an important factor of educational leadership to which future leaders might point with pride.

---

17. Profile, Lucy Fuller James, Itinerant State Teacher Trainer, Vocational Home Economics.

Addenda

ADDENDA

In amassing this material for "The Education of the Negro in North Carolina," the author regrets that many of the facts of educational activities, as well as many who played important roles in them, may have been overlooked or missed entirely. In some cases aid was lacking or material was received too late to be couched in its rightful category. For instance, there is the story of Red Stone Academy, originally known as Bethany School, at Lumberton which was established by a well known Presbyterian minister, the Reverend John H. Hayswood in 1903.

Along with Thompson Institute, headed by W. H. Knuckles, also at Lumberton, Red Stone Academy and Thompson Institute offered the only high school opportunity for Robeson and adjoining counties for many years.

During the early years of the Newbold era, when private secondary schools began to decline, Red Stone was merged with two other Presbyterian schools, Mary Potter Seminary at Oxford and Albion Academy at Franklinton. When the City of Lumberton, like so many other fine cities in the state, assumed its responsibility of giving high school education to Negroes, Red Stone was acquired by the public school system as a high school and Hayswood served as principal until his retirement in 1949.

Dr. G. C. Shaw, who headed Mary Potter Seminary, a fine secondary institution, was succeeded by Herman S. Davis who became principal under the acquisition of Mary Potter into the public school system. Likewise, Albion Academy, long headed by the Reverend John A. Savage, was implemented into the public school system of Franklinton.

Of the many dedicated high school and elementary school principals and teachers, both men and women, an entire book could be written, but that story must be left to some other ambitious scribe who might later chronicle the "Acts of these Apostles" of Negro education.

Let it be hoped that this book will find its way into every public school where Negroes attend that they may ever remember and graciously respect the sublime heritage from which they have sprung and thereby be inspired to erect for posterity "a more stately educational mansion," lest their children shudder at

THE END.

Hugh Victor Brown
Goldsboro, North Carolina
1960

157

Index

159

Dabney, C. W., 44, 45.
Dallas Institute, 28.
Daniel Hand Fund, 27.
Daniels, Frank, 33.
Daniels, Josephus, 33.
Daniel, Robert P., 69, 120.
Daniels, Roscoe, 112.
Davis, George E., 71, 114, 117, 122, 123.
Davis, H. S., 37, 157.
Dawkins, P. W., 82.
Dayton Academy, 27.
Debnam, Frank, 106.
Delaney, Hubert, 70.
Delegate Assembly, NCTA, 119.
De Lomba, Roland, 83.
Department of Agriculture, 125.
Department of Religious Promotion (Shaw), 68.
Dickinson, Sarah, 19.
Dillard, James Hardy, 52, 53, 54.
Dillard High School, 114.
Dillard University, 53.
Division of Negro Education (see Negro Division of Education), 49 52, 59, 61, 65.
Dobbs Farm, 111.
Donnell, 96.
Dorland, Luke, 20, 81, 82, 114.
Dorr, Louise S., 36, 82.
Dortch, William T., 108.
Douglas Academy, 27.
Downing, Lewis K., 72.
Drecher, Julius D., 44.
Dudley, James B., 94, 95.
Dudley, Bishop Thomas, 44.
Duke, B. N., 97, 105.
Duke, Washington, 133.
Dunbar, Paul Lawrence, 17.
Duncan, Ida H., 123.
Duncan, Samuel E., 79, 80, 142, 143.
Dupree, D. D., 130.
Durham, City of, 97, 104, 115, 122.
Dyer Anti-Lynching Bill, 126.

East Piedmont District-NCTA, 119.
Eastern Academy, 27, 39.
Eastern North Carolina Insane Asylum (see State Hospital; Cherry Hospital), 108.
Eaton, H. D., 135.
Edenton Normal and Industrial School, 27.
Edmunds, Helen E., 97.
Educational Governor, 48.
Edwards Brothers, Inc., 153.
Edwards, G. A., 82.
Edwards, Laura L., 111.
Efland Home, 110.
Elder, Alphonse, 99.
Elliott, Charles W., 100.
Eliot, John, 11.

Elizabeth City, N. C., 28, 62, 87.
Elizabeth City Normal (State Teachers College), 32, 69, 84, 87, 89, 142.
Emancipation Proclamation, 16, 17, 21, 26, 67.
Emory University, 43.
Epps, C. M., 123.
Estey Hall, 67.
Estey, Jacob, 67.
Evaluation Criteria, 64.

Faduma, O., 38.
Fairley, R. E., 85.
Faison, Institute, 28.
Faison, J. R., 53.
Faison, W. W., 109.
Farmers Alliance, 95..
Farmers Cooperative Demonstration, 125.
Farm Demonstration Agent, 125.
Faucette, Susie, 82.
Fayetteville, N. C., 30, 32, 33, 76, 85, 87.
Fayetteville State Normal (Teachers College), 69, 72, 84, 85, 87.
Federal Aid,
Ferguson, G. H., 59, 61, 139, 145.
Finger, S. M., 33, 87, 89.
Flowers, J. W., 131.
Foster, J. G. (General), 18.
Foster, Pauline B., 121.
Fountain, Hilda H., 121.
Four-H Clubs, 130, 131, 148.
Franklinton, N. C., 27, 35.
Franklinton Center, 38.
Franklinton County Training School, 150.
Franklinton Normal, 32, 84.
Freedmen's Aid Society, 27.
Freedmen's Board, Presbyterian Church, 27.
Freedmen's Board, United Presbyterian Church, 27, 37.
Freedmen's Bureau, 17, 18, 21, 25, 26, 27, 69, 71, 84.
Free Will Baptist Church, 28.
Friends Society, 27.
Frissell, H. B., 44.
Fusion Politics, 41, 46, 97.

Gaddy, J. W., 110.
Gallaudet College, 105.
Galloway, Margaurite, 130.
Garysburg High School, 28, 35.
General Assembly, 59, 87, 90, 92, 93, 105, 106, 113.
General Education Board, 45, 48, 50, 53, 56, 61, 68, 74.
Ghana, 79.
Gibbon, A. E., 135.
Gibbs, W. T., 96.

161

163

164

Stitt, Neal A. (See
  Acknowledgment).
Stokes, Caroline Phelps, 53.
Strassner, William R., 69.
Suggs, David, 79.
Sutton, Robert B., 70.
Swain, Governor, 13.
Sydenham Hospital, 135.
Synodical Conference of North
  America, 27.

Taft, William H., 57.
Tarpley, J. A., 119.
Tar River Institute, 28.
Tate, Thaddeus L., 106.
Taylor, James R., 151, 153.
Taylor, James T., 99, 122, 123.
Taylor, Salomie, 135.
Technical Institute, 153.
Tennessee A. and I. University, 76,
  87, 103.
Texas Southern University, 83.
Thayer, Edward O., 73.
Thirteenth Amendment, 21.
Thomas, Roy, 147.
Thompson, A. H., 36.
Thompson Institute, 28, 36.
Tillett, J. J., 110.
Tolliver, Frank A., 144.
Townsville Mission, 27.
Trent, William J., 79.
Trent, W. J., Jr., 79.
Trigg, Frank, 74.
Trigg, Harold L., 70, 90, 123, 141, 142.
Trinity College (Duke University),
  134.
Troy, N. C., 26, 38.
Tryon, N. C., 27.
Tupper, Henry Martin, 19, 20, 22, 31,
  67, 69, 114, 115.
Turner, J. T., 106.
Turner, W. S., 116, 123.
Tuskegee Institute, 50, 57, 103, 134.

Umstead, John, 111, 112.
Union Academy, 28.
United Negro College Fund, 68, 70,
  79, 81.
U. S. Office of Education, 53.
Universal Education, 26, 40, 42, 44,
  47, 48, 49.
University of Chicago, 153.
University of Hamburg, 110.
University of Hawaii, 76.
University of North Carolina, 93.
University of Pittsburgh, 87, 103.

Vance, Zebulon, 107.
Varser, Judge, 106.
Verner, A. W., 82.

Virginia Randolph Fund, 53.
Vitolls, M. M., 109.

Wade, Lucy, 130.
Wagram, N. C., 160.
Walden, R. I., 35.
Wallace, J. E., 74.
Walls, W. J., 76, 79.
Walters, Alexander, 79.
Warren, J. W., Jr., 148, 151.
Warren, S. L., 133.
Warrenton, 35.
Warrick, William, 114.
Washburn Seminary, 26.
Washington, Booker T., 57, 103, 128.
Washington, D. C., 31, 69, 72, 96.
Washington, George, 17.
Washington High, Raleigh, 82.
Washington, N. C., 16, 17, 19, 29, 34.
Washington and Lee College, 13, 52.
Waters Institute, 26, 28, 35.
Waters, William, 112.
Wayne County, 135.
Webster, Daniel, 49.
Weeks, A. L. E., 37.
Weeks, Stephen B., 14.
Weldon, N. C., 28, 35.
Wentz, S. F., 38.
West Charlotte High School, 199.
Western District, NCTA, 118, 119.
West Point, N. Y., 19.
Whaley, Ruth Whitehead, 79.
Wharton Institute, 28.
Wheeler, J. T., 82.
Whelpley, F. L., 109.
Whitaker, Albert, 110.
White, Evelyn Davidson, 82.
White, George N., 46.
Whiteville, N. C., 150.
Whitfield, G. R., 53.
Whitehead, Matthew, 72.
Whitted, Bessie Alberta, 82.
Whitted, Ruby, 112.
Who's Who in Agriculture, 128.
Wilberforce University, 147.
Wilder, Bessie, 93.
Wiley, C. H., 114.
Williams, Charlie, 106.
Williams, George H., 85.
Williams, J. S., 82.
Williams, Malcolm, 87.
Williams, M. M., 165.
Williams, M. W., 106.
Williams, Roger, 11.
Williams, S. D., 119, 123.
Williams, Sarah, 130.
Willimantic State Teachers College,
  92.
Williston, of Massachusetts, 38.
Wilmington, City of, 16, 26, 30, 38, 46,
  134, 135.
Wilmington Normal, 38.

166

Wilson, A. J., 135.
Wilson, M. L., 90.
Wilson, N. C., 34.
Winston, Ellen, 111.
Winston-Salem, City of, 32, 44, 62, 97, 114.
Winston-Salem Slater Normal Teachers College), 84, 90, 92, 93, 103.
Winton, N. C., 26, 35.

Woman's Home Mission Society, Methodist Church, 74.
Woodson, Minnie Lawrence, 145, 146.
Wortham, James L., 14.
Wright, E. O., 36.
Wynn, R. L., 131.

Young, William J., 105.

Zion Academy, 28.
Zion Wesley Institute, 76, 78.